The Unequal Struggle?

British socialism and the
capitalist enterprise

The Unequal Struggle?

British socialism and the capitalist enterprise

JIM TOMLINSON

METHUEN

LONDON AND NEW YORK

First published in 1982 by
Methuen & Co. Ltd
11 New Fetter Lane, London EC4P 4EE

Published in the USA by
Methuen & Co.
in association with Methuen, Inc.
733 Third Avenue, New York, NY 10017

Printed in Great Britain at the
University Press, Cambridge

British Library Cataloguing in Publication Data

Tomlinson, Jim
The unequal struggle?
1. Capitalism
I. Title
330.12'2   HB501
ISBN 0-416-33150-5
ISBN 0-416-33160-2 Pbk

Library of Congress Cataloging in Publication Data

Tomlinson, Jim.
The unequal struggle?
Bibliography: p.
Includes index.
1. Government business enterprises – Great
Britain.   2. Government ownership – Great Britain.
3. Employees' representation in management – Great
Britain.   4. Socialism – Great Britain.
5. Marxian economics.   I. Title.
HD4145.T6 1982   338.941'04   82-7885
ISBN 0-416-33150-5   AACR2
ISBN 0-416-33160-2 (pbk.)

Contents

Acknowledgements

This book has benefited greatly from discussions in the Conference of Socialist Economists' 'Money' Group, especially with Stuart Burchell and Grahame Thompson, and in the Birkbeck College Seminar on 'Politics and the State'. John Whitehead has read the whole manuscript and provided comments which have been invaluable in turning a rather ill-organized manuscript into what I hope is something approaching a book. The style of the book has also been greatly improved by the comments of Kathryn Tomlinson.

Chris Newnham typed several drafts of the manuscript with her customary speed and efficiency.

Introduction

Like many books this one has arisen primarily from a feeling of dissatisfaction, in this case with the way in which certain kinds of political arguments are conducted. The political arguments are those conducted by socialists in relation to what is perhaps the most important institution of the capitalist economy, the enterprise. The object of this book is to argue why dissatisfaction is an appropriate response and to try and make suggestions as to how such discussions might be more satisfactorily conducted.

Perhaps this dissatisfaction can best be illustrated in relation to something which is currently very much a central issue for socialist politics – the 'Alternative Economic Strategy' (AES). This strategy, in its various forms, touches on almost every aspect of the economy, but it is where it impinges upon notions of the enterprise that is of concern here. This takes place at two particular points – in the discussion of nationalization, and the discussion of industrial democracy (the latter, as argued later, largely subsuming the question of planning agreements).

The discussion of nationalization in the AES is characterized on the one hand by a commitment to its extension but on the other by a strong hostility to the current form of public corporation (CSE/LWG 1980, pp. 74–5; Aaronovitch 1981, pp. 52–62). Now this combination is not of itself surprising, but what is surprising is that it is not tied to *any* detailed analysis of nationalization as a form of socialist policy. Thus the AES proposes an organizationally different kind of nationalization but characterizes this simply in terms of involving 'industrial democracy' (Aaronovitch 1981, p. 52) or 'production for social need and democratic forms of management' (CSE/LWG, p. 74). These vague slogans are symptomatic of the extraordinary neglect which nationalization has suffered at the hands of British socialism. As two socialists have recently commented: 'we find little analysis of nationalization at either a theoretical or empirical level' (Fine and O'Donnell 1981, p. 265). Discussion of nationalization by socialists has tended to be dominated by a crude functionalism, with nationalization a way of providing 'goods and services necessary for the reproduction of the system that cannot be provided either effectively or profitably by competitive private capital' (Aaronovitch and Smith 1981, p. 126). This is coupled with a critique of the existing nationalized industries which mainly stresses that they have been effectively 'recapitalised' (e.g. Fine and O'Donnell). But what is almost entirely absent is any account of how nationalized industries might be run in the future beyond the invocation of 'democracy' and 'social need'. Yet many of the problems which have arisen in the running of nationalized industries in Britain over the last thirty-five years would recur under almost any conceivable political framework. Problems of investment levels, pricing policy, management structure, relations of the industry to the appropriate government ministry – all these and a host of other problems cannot be conjured away by 'democracy'. Of course these issues have been exhaustively discussed in Britain – but not by socialists. The great majority of socialists have maintained an Olympian detachment from the debates over these issues in Britain – leaving the field free for economists, civil servants, conservatives and a few social democrats.

We thus have socialists remaining committed to nationalization but having extraordinarily little to say on how the enterprises to be nationalized are to be run. Two points of importance follow from this. First the disquiet over nationalization has *not* led to its repudiation as an objective. Yet it is clear that this adoption as *the* socialist objective, especially in the form of Clause IV of the Labour Party constitution, was a result of highly particular features of the time when this adoption took place, 1918.

First it is worth stressing that when the constitution, including Clause IV, was originally brought in, this clause was a very minor part of the discussions that went on. The bulk of the discussion at the 1918 conferences that adopted the constitution was about the reorganization of the party onto an individual membership basis, which aroused a lot of hostility from the trade unions (see Labour Party 1918; McKibbin 1974, pp. 91–106). Not only was nationalization *not* the central feature of the constitution as seen at the time, but its inclusion indicated not an extended reflection on the nature of socialist policies but rather a variety of short-term, *ad hoc* points. Partly it was felt electorally desirable to sharpen the difference between Liberal and Labour parties by stressing such a principle, as well as offering a vaguely formulated 'umbrella' to the heterogeneous components of the Labour Party (McKibbin, pp. 96–7). Some saw common ownership as a slogan to appeal to the middle classes (ibid., p. 97) whilst others saw it as reflecting the success of the nationalizations of the Russian Revolution. In addition the domestic political context, of a successful extension of state control during the war, seemed to show that nationalization had proved its worth (Barry, p. 200).

This historical specificity of nationalization as a socialist objective is stressed to bring out the lack of an obvious general link between socialism and nationalization. Indeed even in Britain this equation did not come to the centre of the politics of the Left until after the Second World War, when the forces behind the traditional claims for nationalization (notably of the mines and railways) were satisfied by the acts of the 1945–51 Labour government, and the question of the further extension of such measures became a crucial political issue.

The second point about the absence of discussion of the organizational forms of nationalization by the British Left is that it has left a gaping void (or perhaps rather a few slogans) where a 'politics of the enterprise' should have been. The Left has not dirtied its hands by examining all those gritty but crucial problems about financial control, information systems, organizational hierarchies, accounting methods, etc. which *any* serious proposals for enterprise reform would have to deal with. Rather there has been a general retreat into utopianism, in which all these problems will be abolished once the appointed day of true socialism arrives.

A central slogan of the AES is industrial democracy or its synonym workers' control (CSE/LWG 1980, pp. 79–82; Aaronovitch 1981, pp. 71–4). Yet again it must be said that the discussion of this objective is characterized by remarkably little organizational detail. The reasons for its desirability are stated, some problems pointed out and a rather rapid skating over any particular proposals (especially those of the

3

Bullock Committee) is given. In some ways it is the latter which in a sense gives the game away. For the discussion of any particular form of industrial democracy must rapidly reveal the poverty of the concepts which socialists normally bring to bear in this area. A few slogans serve to avoid any useful discussions. For example, in the CSE/LWG version of the AES the dangers of enterprise 'syndicalism' and 'incorporation' are suggested (see also Chapter 2). These 'antislogans' serve as warnings of the dangers of too much worker control outside the context of a planned economy. Yet a major specific proposal of the AES is for planning agreements, which if taken seriously would mean a great extension of 'incorporation' by involving the workforce directly in corporate decision-making. Such a consequence would be little offset by the capacities of the government to effect decisions at enterprise level envisaged in the AES. These would amount to little more than the rather ineffective financial benefits and penalties operated by most post-war governments in Britain.[1]

I

The above points are offered as examples of the unsatisfactory way enterprises have been discussed in the AES. This is not something peculiar to the AES but a much more general problem. This book tries to get to grips with the problem. It does so by focusing on a variety of socialist arguments that have been deployed concerning the capitalist enterprise.[2]

'Socialist' is used in a broad but conventional way to describe those writers who have given themselves such a label. But of course a book which attempted to cover everything said by socialists about the capitalist enterprise would run to many thousands of (albeit repetitive) pages. Clearly, therefore, some principles of selection have had to be used to provide a manageable amount of material. These principles have been two – theoretical importance and political impact.

The first principle is based on the view that *one* element which the analysis of any political arguments should examine is the coherence and subtlety of their theoretical positions and the ability of these positions to open up new lines of intelligibility concerning phenomena. Such a view is in turn founded upon the belief that theoretical arguments are vital to politics, indeed that political activity is always predicated upon explicit or implicit conceptions irreducible to 'experience' or its synonyms. This is true of such 'obvious' categories as

4

nationalization and democracy, discussed above. This point is probably unexceptionable to all but the most diehard empiricists, but it carries its own dangers, above all the danger of an overly 'rationalist' conception of politics where the best arguments decide the battles. But the pen is not mightier than the sword. This means that a second criterion, that of 'political impact', has been employed. The use of such a criterion is intended to register the existence and often long-term survival within socialist arguments of positions which seem theoretically poorly equipped to bear the political weight placed upon them. In other words there is no mechanism within political argument whereby only the 'fittest' survive – and this of course a point by no means confined to *socialist* political argument.

A problem with the use of these two distinct principles of selection is of course that they may not be compatible. In the case of Marx (as is further argued below), his arguments must clearly be included on both grounds. All but the most philistine now seem to accept the theoretical importance of his work, and the political impact is of course not by any means limited to those who call themselves Marxists. For several others discussed in this book the two criteria are not in accord. The Webbs, for example, whatever their strengths (particularly their extraordinary ability to marshal mountains of institutional material to make a case), cannot be thought of as very profound theoreticians. One may even suggest that their political volatility, notably their late conversion to Stalinism, was in part an effect of the absence of much in the way of theoretical anchoring. Yet despite (or perhaps because of?) this they have exerted an enormous influence on British socialism, if to a considerable extent in a negative fashion by provoking attempts to refute them. There is something similar in the cases of Crosland and Holland. The second of these two authors raises a further general problem about the format of this book. Holland's work, I would suggest, has had a great political impact on British socialism not through any great novelty of argument but rather because it has skilfully drawn together and perhaps given a particular twist to certain themes which have long played a considerable role in socialist argument. Holland's writings acted to crystallize and to some extent formalize positions with long pedigrees within British socialism. This function of 'crystallizing' generally prevalent arguments justifies focusing on this particular author what may appear to be disproportionate amounts of critical attention. I have taken this author as broadly representative of arguments which did not have their origins primarily in his work.

This manner of treating the various authors – as 'representatives' of important socialist arguments concerning the enterprise – means that no attempt is being made to give a rounded account of every aspect of their work. For example Crosland is of course important for many other things than his discussion of the managerial revolution – ideologically the stress on equality as the prime socialist objective has been equally significant, and perhaps equally problematic (see Rose 1980).

A slightly different problem arises where there is no such 'representative' author who has elaborated and formalized widely circulating arguments. Thus in Chapter 2 there has been no one author who could be referred to who has at any length put the Marxist case against co-operatives and workers on the board of capitalist enterprises. In the absence of such work a wide range of authors are cited who may be said to have collectively elaborated certain positions which are implicit in much of their individual work.

One final point on the general format of this book concerns its concentration on *British* socialism. This focus is based not on any disregard for the theoretical weight or political impact of other socialisms, but the belief that British socialism remains largely *sui generis*, relatively immune from foreign, especially non-English-speaking, influences. This is not based, I would argue, on a simple chauvinistic reflex (though this is certainly not absent – see for example Thompson 1978) but partly on the linguistic and cultural barriers to the importation of European socialist thought (despite the attempts of *New Left Review* in particular), and above all on the national character of almost all socialist political organization in the UK, the latter being something so far little altered by participation in the politics of the European parliament. There are markedly few systematic organizational links between British and any other socialism to provide channels whereby this 'isolationism' would be broken down, in the way that for example the Third International acted as a channel for the dissemination of Bolshevism. This ideological insularity is perhaps also illustrated by the resilience of British socialism to the importation of 'alien' institutions like the National Enterprise Board. This, modelled on the Italian Industrial Reorganization Institution, could find no secure home in a different political climate, that is one dominated by disputes over public versus private ownership.[3]

Socialist ideology has traditionally been dominated by questions of economic relations. This has commonly derived from a conception that the shape of 'society as a whole' is based primarily on economic relations – that is the primacy of the economy has been linked to an ontology of society. This is of course very explicit in Marxism with its base/superstructure notion which, whatever its many and widely acknowledged shortcomings, does provide a crudely appropriate metaphor for Marxist approaches to society. Non-Marxist socialism has been less explicitly clear as to the reasons for the primacy of the economic, but has commonly implicitly conceded it, if only in some vague belief that for example most social problems (inequality, employment, health, education) can only be adequately tackled if the economy is 'got right' first.

Such a primacy of the economic does not necessarily depend on ontologies. It can be constructed simply as a result of a 'political calculation', i.e. that from the point of vision of socialist politics the economy is the most important and/or most tractable area of social relations. Thus the contestation of Marxist ontologies does not of itself involve any necessary reduction in the *political* primacy of the economic (Cutler *et al.* 1977, 1978).

Whatever the basis of this primacy it would perhaps be thought to have led to a large literature dealing at length and in detail with the capitalist enterprise as the primary unit in the organization of the capitalist economy. On the whole this has *not* been the case. Whilst there is of course a great deal of socialist literature on the capitalist economy, comprehensive accounts of the capitalist enterprise from a socialist position are few and far between. Again there are of course numerous accounts dealing with particular aspects of the enterprise. In recent years, especially following Braverman's (1974) account of the monopoly capital labour process, for example, there has been an explosion in the literature on the capitalist labour process ('Braver-mania') which now also seems to be taking on an increasingly historical dimension (e.g. Samuel 1977; Berg 1979). Equally there is a considerable literature on the modern enterprise conceived as a monopoly (e.g. Baran and Sweezy 1968; Aaronovitch and Sawyer 1975). Both of these approaches are discussed in this book. But whatever the intrinsic merits or otherwise of these approaches they remain necessarily partial. There are relatively few attempts at a socialist 'overview' of the capitalist enterprise. The closest to such an overview probably comes in the form of a radical sociology of work organizations and the enterprise (e.g. Salaman 1979, 1981). The central thrust of such works is to 'sociologize' the enterprise away into the surrounding society. 'Throughout, it will be maintained that internal aspects of employing organizations can only be understood in terms of their location within capitalist societies' (1979, p. 34). Whatever qualifications are inserted, such conceptions of the capitalist enterprise must always slide off into general discussions of class structure, power, ideology and all the other themes of Weberian and Marxist sociology, leaving the enterprise as little more than a relay for forces constructed and battling elsewhere, that is little *in particular* is said about the enterprise.

General notions of the enterprise are thus dominated by non-socialist conceptions. This perhaps is particularly surprising given the centrality of discussion of the enterprise to recent proposals for economic reform in the existing socialist countries (e.g. Granick 1976).

This book grew out of a dissatisfaction with political arguments outlined above plus a desire to see what kind of shape such an overview of the capitalist enterprise might have. It is of course only a preliminary attempt, an attempt to review the main lines of argument, not a comprehensive treatise.

Its starting point is a discussion of Marxist socialist discussions of the enterprise. This starting point is justifiable on two counts. First, the majority of existing socialist literature on this, as on many other subjects, is organized around for or against Marxism. I have attempted to discuss Marx and Marxism whilst escaping this dichotomy both by restricting the discussion of Marxism to only a small part of the total positions available, and by stressing that even within this restricted area the Marxist legacy is a heterogeneous, complex and often contradictory one, impossible to embrace or reject *in toto*.

Second, Marxism was the actual starting point of the author. The first two chapters may be read as an attempt to come to terms with the perceived inadequacies of Marxism for the purposes of socialist politics. The first chapter attempts to show some of the problems raised by Marx's analysis of the enterprise in *Capital*. The second attempts to link two recent socialist arguments relating to the enterprise by their origins to Marxism, and to argue there are problems with many parts of these arguments. It should be stressed here that the suggestion is *not* that the arguments that socialists brought to bear on the recent disputes discussed were simply derived from Marx, that is purely logical consequences of the positions of *Capital* and other of this works. This would be an example of the 'rationalism' argued against already. Clearly almost any political argument reflects the complicated exigencies of the moment and is not simply derived from general theories. Nevertheless the argument is that these arguments *were* heavily impregnated with Marxist (or at least Marxian) positions and that this is a problem.

The bulk of the remainder of the book is concerned with the analysis of the capitalist enterprise produced by British non-Marxist socialists. This is not meant as a comprehensive account of guild socialism, Fabianism, Revisionism, etc. The focus throughout is the attempt to draw out from these discussions arguments which still appear pertinent to socialist ideology because of their theoretical substance or political impact. This no doubt involves doing violence to the 'contexts' in which these various positions were produced. But there is no necessary reason why we should privilege these contexts in discussing such arguments. The implications of the arguments for socialist ideology are independent of the 'period', the 'thought of X' or other means commonly used to contextualize theories. We may for example be interested in the early twentieth-century background to G.D.H. Cole's work, his arguments on other topics, his psychic state when talking about industrial democracy, etc., but none of this need be relevant to an evaluation of his arguments. The criterion I have used – that of importance in some long-term way to socialist ideology – is of course itself extremely contentious – itself part of a never resolvable political argument. But such open-endedness of argument seems preferable to reducing Cole's or anyone else's arguments merely to 'reflections' of something else – material conditions, an essence of mind, a psyche or whatever.

The second part of the book, Chapters 3 to 6, is arranged in a rough chronological order, but this is an organizational convenience and carries no implication of evolution within the arguments.

Chapter 3 focuses on what remains the most important discussion of industrial democracy in British socialism, the dispute between Cole and the Webbs. Many more recent arguments in this area have been only pale and partial re-runs of this dispute, often not reflecting the central role of political theory in the discussion of industrial democracy.

Chapter 4 discusses what, in a British context, can perhaps be called the socialist gut reaction to the capitalist enterprise – nationalization. The limitations of this 'panacea', what is at best its only partial relevance to socialist objectives, are suggested here particularly in relation to the creation of the typical British form of organization of nationalized industries, the public corporation.

Chapter 5 looks at the post-1945 disputes over the 'managerial revolution' in which socialist revisionists attempted to link changes in the character of the capitalist enterprise to changes in capitalism in general. Many of the points raised by this argument remain largely unsettled but are nevertheless important, not least because of the central part played in the argument by the role of management, the analysis of which has always been a major weakness of socialist accounts of the enterprise.

Chapter 6 focuses on the most recent attempts on the Left to theorize about the capitalist enterprise and link changes in those enterprises to capitalism as a whole. This discussion remains the implicit or explicit foundation of much of the contemporary Left's position.

The final chapter attempts to draw together the threads of the previous chapters and to build on some of the positive points made in those chapters. This involves emphasizing the complex problem of the nature and status of socialist objectives *vis-à-vis* the enterprise, which in turn requires a wide-ranging discussion of socialist ideology in general.

NOTES

1 I owe this point directly to Stuart Burchell.
2 Of course the notion of 'capitalist enterprise' is highly ambiguous and this is much more than just a terminological problem. It is taken up at some length in Chapter 7.
3 Though the idea of the NEB also owed a great deal to Crosland's (1956) work.

CHAPTER ONE

Marx's *Capital* and the analysis of the capitalist enterprise

The purpose of this chapter is to outline and criticize the conceptions of the capitalist enterprise at work in Marx's *Capital*. Within socialist arguments Marx's formulations play a fundamental role, even in the arguments of those who would not at all consider themselves Marxists. This is not to suggest that socialist arguments on the enterprise are ever simply deductions from Marx's (or anybody else's) theories: all kinds of other exigencies enter. This point applies to Marx himself – his political position on policies on the enterprise are not deduced from, and may actually contradict, the general theoretical formulations. This seems to be the case for example in his discussions of the Factory Acts (see below). Nevertheless theoretical positions necessarily inform political arguments and practice and for this reason and because of the role of Marxism in socialist ideology the arguments of Marx's *Capital* are the best starting point for this book.

I

At the most general level the concepts of *Capital* do not construct a theory of the enterprise as such. This is because Marx treats individual capitals as merely representatives, as 'aliquot parts', of the total social capital. Therefore much of the argument is at the level of the laws of motion and tendencies of capital as a generality, with particular capitals subsumed within this. However, in this area as elsewhere in *Capital*, there are multiple levels of analysis, and Marx at different points in the text puts forward disparate elements which could be said to provide the basis for a theory of the enterprise. These elements are the concepts of the centralization, concentration and socialization of capital; the despotism of capital or of the factory; fetishism; and the labour process. I will first outline Marx's arguments concerning these elements and the overall conception of the enterprise which flows from them, and then raise the problems of each in turn.

Centralization and concentration of capital are the terms which Marx used to analyse changes in the *size* of the enterprise (Marx 1954, pp. 586–9, 714–5). The centralization process is that whereby a given total capital is more and more fused into a smaller number of units as a result of competition. Concentration is the growth in size brought about by the expansion of existing capitals – their extended reproduction. The processes reinforce each other and from them Marx constructs an unconditional tendency towards a 'constantly diminishing number of the magnates of capital' (Marx 1954, p. 715).

Although the tendency is unconditional, Marx does not present it as leading to a smooth linear progress. Quite the contrary, the tendency is seen as a theoretical necessity, but also as an *historical* one involving class struggles, inter-capitalist competition and periodic crises which interrupt its progress. Nevertheless, despite all these obstacles the tendency grinds on – it is interrupted only to be inevitably continued. What Marx calls the 'empirical limits' can only delay the tendency. It cannot be stopped. Marx's conception is faithfully summarized by Poulantzas (1975, p. 145 n.): 'I should like to recall here that the concentration and centralization of capital should in no way be seen, in its real historical development, as a gradual, unlinear and homogeneous process. In certain periods, generally brief, this process can even undergo relative retreats.'

Legal changes in the enterprise, especially the growth of joint stock companies, are largely seen as part of this concentration/ centralization process (Marx 1972, pp. 436–41). Marx argues that the formation of joint stock companies facilitates 'an enormous expansion of the scale of production and of enterprises, that was impossible for individual capitals' (1972, p. 436). Further, within the legal form of the joint stock company the process of socialization proceeds – the growth of integration and co-operation within production which presages socialism. Thus the legal status of the enterprise is conceived as both functional to an inescapable process of capitalism, and as called into being by that process.

12

It is also largely in relation to the processes of centralization and concentration of capital that Marx's analysis of credit is organized. In his analysis of the role of credit Marx (1972, Ch. xxvii) distinguishes several elements, but the stress is on credit's role in the formation of joint stock companies which then feeds into the lines of argument noted in the previous paragraph.

Centralization and concentration are also the basis of Marx's conception of the growth of industrial 'monopoly' (especially 1972, pp. 437–8). Three points are worth stressing in this context. First Marx does not offer a systematic discussion of industrial monopoly in *Capital* – most of the discussion of this concept relates to a different problem entirely, that of *landed* property. Second many attempts to systematize Marx's few comments on industrial monopoly rapidly become very difficult to distinguish from neo-classical conceptions. For example if one takes Sweezy's account (1968, Chs xiv and xv), one of the most systematic and best known, the argument could be almost entirely re-written using neo-classical terms without fundamentally changing the nature of the argument. Monopoly raises prices, and profits are increased at the expense of either non-monopoly sectors or wages. Also by 'barriers to entry' profit levels in different industries are not as readily equalized as under competitive conditions. Monopolists under-invest in their own sectors in order to maintain the marginal rate of profit. Monopoly causes the costs of distribution to be increased. The argument would differ from that of neo-classical economists only in relation to the role of monopoly in accelerating 'the falling rate of profit' (p. 277). But this effect is the result of the assertion that monopoly increases accumulation of capital because 'the proportion accumulated increases with the segment of surplus value' (p. 274) which is simply asserted. Also more generally it means that the only specifically 'Marxist' effect of monopoly in this account is tied to that most problematic notion, the tendency of the rate of profit to fall.

Sweezy's discussion of monopoly could be said to arise from the ambiguity of the word. Also the ease with which monopoly in Marxism becomes seemingly inextricably entangled with what are presumably wholly alien concepts, such as those of neo-classical economics, is linked to the fact that in that framework monopoly has in principle a much more clear-cut meaning. Some of the ambiguity of the concept of monopoly and the problems this causes for socialist argument are taken up in Chapter 6 below.

Probably the most sustained attempt to discuss monopoly in a rigorously Marxist framework which evades these ambiguities is that of Poulantzas (1975). His general argument is that monopoly can have a meaning for Marxism only in so far as it alters the relations of production. He argues that there is no fundamental transformation of the labour process in the movement from competitive to monopoly capitalism – the form of the labour process was fundamentally changed during the 'manufacture' stage and this core of a socialized labour process does not alter under capitalism.

The transformation of the relations of production under monopoly capitalism is therefore characterized 'by differential forms of the dominant capitalist relations of production' (p. 117), changes in the form of appropriation of surplus value. These changes in form correspond to a rise in the rate of exploitation designed to counteract the tendency for the average rate of profit to fall. These changes are directly reflected in (p. 118):

1 changes in legal ownership;
2 changes in the boundaries of production units;
3 differentiation between the agents of capital.

The current phase of monopoly capitalism is then seen as one in which the units of possession are once again becoming coterminous with units of ownership which had tended to become disassociated in the first phase. In other words the boundaries of the enterprise change to bring the organization and direction of the labour process in line with the unit of ownership. In the end the processes outlined by Poulantzas are 'expressions' of the tendency towards the merging of capitals, i.e. once again we are back to the complex appearances of the underlying tendency towards concentration and centralization (p. 127). Poulantzas does warn (especially pp. 138–9) against the use of size criteria in dividing monopoly from non-monopoly capital, but his central argument is against the political 'errors' that the use of size criteria may lead to rather than their complete theoretical inadequacy. This is not to deny the importance of some of the tendencies discussed by Poulantzas, but to question their unification into something called *monopoly* which then generates a constant slippage towards talk of size.

Finally it is clear from the above that what is explicitly Marxist in most analyses of monopoly is related to the *size* of firms. Monopolies arise when the average size of individual capitals increases. If this is the case 'monopoly' does not need to be assessed separately from the concepts of centralization and concentration which are also about size. More importantly this further implies that the notion of 'monopoly capitalism' as a stage of capitalism should be abandoned, because as Hussain (1976, p. 8) notes, 'The size of the firm cannot serve as the basis of periodisation because capitalism does not put any *a priori* restriction on the scale of production and consequently the size of the firm.'

These concepts of Marx have a number of implications, but here I want just to note that they have the consequence of homogenizing the form of enterprises. Both size and legal status are seen as changing sequentially, so that differences in size and legal status are merely signs of differential progress along the same road. Coexisting permanent (or lasting) differences in size and legal status are strictly speaking theoretically unthinkable; what happens to each enterprise is simply a representation of what is happening to the social capital as a whole.

The second element of the analysis of the enterprise Marx presents is that of the 'despotism of the factory' (Marx 1954, pp. 313–14). The despotism of the factory is derived by Marx from the dual character of capitalist production.

> If, then, the control of the capitalist is in substance two-fold by reason of the two-fold nature of the process of production itself – which on the one hand, is a social process for producing use-values, on the other a process for creating surplus value – in form that control is despotic. (p. 314)

This dual character of capitalist production is stressed by Marx to contradict those political economists who would conflate the two. Both aspects create a need for despotism. The production of use-values requires despotism because of the need to co-ordinate the efforts of diverse labourers in a co-operative process, the production of surplus value likewise because of the antagonism it generates between workers and capitalists. So whilst production retains either of these characteristics it must remain despotic.[1]

The theory of fetishism provides a third element in Marx's conceptualization of the enterprise (Marx 1972, Chs 1 and 2). Fetishism is the way Marx thinks capitalists (as well as other agents) calculate. Whilst for Marx the rate of profit depends on the extraction of surplus value, and therefore what matters is the amount of variable capital and the rate of exploitation, the capitalist calculates as if all costs of production were equivalent in producing profit – so he calculates profit as the difference between total cost prices and total selling prices. 'So far as the individual capitalist is concerned, it is evident that he is only interested in the relation of the surplus value, or the excess value at which he sells his commodities, to the total capital advanced for the production of commodities' (1972, p. 43) and that 'the relationships of capital are obscured by the fact that all parts of capital appear equally as the source of excess value (profit)' (1972, p. 45). But this form of calculation is not of course just an illusion, an error. The form of calculation is necessary for the reproduction of capital, because the capitalist must indeed replace his costs of production if production is to continue (pp. 36–7).[2]

Thus fetishism provides a means of thinking about capitalist calculation which makes this form of calculation a necessary effect of capitalism – the capitalist must calculate this way because he is a capitalist. This calculation in turn is absolutely necessary for the continuation of capitalism – it reproduces one of capitalism's conditions of existence. This dual conception of capitalist calculation as both effect of and condition of existence of capitalism is of course precisely what is brilliant in Marx's notion of fetishism.

The final element significant for Marx's analysis of the enterprise is the concept of the labour process. In analysing production Marx privileges labour for two reasons. One is because of his conception of labour as the source of surplus value, labour as the irreducible element in capitalist production. The second reason is because of his conception of production as something in which man acts on the material world, and in doing so changes himself. 'By thus acting on the external world and changing it, he at the same time changes his own nature' (Marx 1954, p. 173). From this privileging of labour Marx can then conceive capitalist production as generating certain tendencies primarily in relation to labour, above all the separation of mental and manual labour and the subordination of labour to the machine[3] (e.g. Marx 1954, pp. 398–9).

To summarize so far, we can say that Marx's general conception is of capitalist enterprises which are organizationally homogeneous, rigidly hierarchical and despotic, which calculate in ways determined by capitalist relations of production in general, and which can best be analysed in terms of a *labour* process. Each of these points will be taken in turn and some of the problems of each suggested.

16

II

The conception of tendencies towards the socialization of the enterprises under capitalism can be criticized in a number of ways. Cutler *et al.* (1977, 1978) have criticized Marx's general concept of tendencies operative within the capitalist mode of production. For example they have pointed out Marx's variant conceptions of these tendencies, and how some of them are indeterminant in the sense of being compatible with any state of the world (because the effects of the tendencies, if not apparent, can always be said to be for the moment counteracted)[4] or incoherent in Marx's own terms in the sense of conflating analysis at the level of a mode of production with that at the level of a social formation, which is always a combination of elements of different modes of production. A third kind of tendency is one which, like that of centralization/concentration/socialization, is not realized unproblematically (Cutler *et al.* 1977, pp. 132–4) in the sense of having 'empirical limits', but nevertheless is always ultimately achieved. The difficulty with this sort of tendency is that it depends on the notion that the form of integration of production under capitalism is unaffected by capitalism itself. Within the shell of capitalist production develops a proto-socialist economy awaiting only a breaking of the shell to reveal the kernel of ongoing socialization. This position cannot be assailed on logical grounds, but its implications for socialists are bizarre. It implies that the particular kinds of markets served, the commodity form of production employed, the managerial practices employed, etc. by capitalist firms don't really matter because socialization is continuing in any case. All differences are subsumed under this over-arching tendency. Capitalism *may* exhibit strong tendencies to increasing division of labour and integration of production, but the form of this integration cannot be separated off from the other practices embodied in the firm. Integration is affected by, for example, the need for financial reproduction of the enterprise (see Chapter 7), and the forms of hierarchy of management, neither of which can be treated as 'shell' simply to be broken off revealing an untarnished kernel of socialist relations of production.

Equally, Marx's mode of analysis cannot avoid making any changes in, for example, company law both functional and largely unimportant. Functional because called into being by the 'needs' of capital – the need for concentration and centralization; largely unimportant because they only provide a 'shell' within which the

17

kernel has an almost independent existence. Under the joint stock form of private property the socialization of production marches on in the same way, if more rapidly than it had previously.

If we disregard Marx's analysis of the significance of changes in the size and legal status of enterprises we open up a number of important questions which his theoretical analysis tends to suppress. First we can simply ask: what is the pertinence of the size of the enterprise for socialists? If the increase in size of enterprises is no longer read as progressive because it is linked to the 'development of the forces of production' and socialization then it is possible to argue for example that capitalist enterprises should be broken up to facilitate that standard socialist objective, worker control of enterprises. In the Marxist framework sketched above this would seem both utopian and reactionary. Utopian because it tries to prevent the ineluctable tendencies of concentration and centralization; reactionary because it cuts across the socialization of production, in which history is definitely on the side of socialism.

However, that the breaking up of capitalist enterprises would be possible *without* making impossible certain types of existing production process is strongly suggested by Prais (1976). He points out that the major reason for the growth of large enterprises (legally defined units) in Britain has been the rise of the multi-plant enterprise, growth in the size of plants being much less important, i.e. concentration has not largely been caused by the 'socialization' of production in so far as this is represented by growth of plant size. This argument is not intended as support for the romanticization of 'small business' current on the Right, but simply as an example of what is open to debate once Marx's position of treating changes in the size of enterprise as simply part of an inevitable and progressive tendency is no longer followed. (On this see Chapters 3 and 7 and also Tomlinson 1980a.)

The legal status of the enterprise can be opened up in the same way. Marxists have commonly treated the form of company law as irrelevant because of their conception of property as essentially either private or public, and this devalues differences in the *form* of private property.[5] This is tied to an 'essentialist' notion of law in which property rights are conceived of as giving an unambiguous control of means of production. If these means are in private hands this gives these private owners control over their use and disposition. If they are in public hands one clear agency of control is displaced by another. This conception of property rights raises the problems that (a) rights of possession in law are always particular rights, constrained in their exercise by both the laws which construct these rights and other laws, and (b) the use of means of production is constrained by a variety of non-legal practices. Let us consider each of these in turn. A British joint stock company is currently constrained in a number of ways in the disposition of its assets (see Hadden 1977). For example it has to use them for objectives defined in the company's articles of association; it has to use them for the benefit of members of the company; and it has to maintain its capital intact. Outside the framework of company law companies are constrained to a variety of degrees by Factory Acts, Health and Safety Acts, Employment Protection Acts and a host of other legislation. These current legal constraints have of course been historically formed, but there was *never* a time when constraints in general were absent. The law may be strong in the defence of the rights of private property, but these rights are always particular ones. (The recent political importance of differences in the form of company law is taken up in Chapter 2 below.)

The non-legal constraints on possession in the enterprise are taken up below in discussing 'the despotism of capital'.

As noted above Marx's thesis of the despotism of capital has a two-fold derivation – from the nature of the labour process and from the production of commodities. The need for co-ordination in modern industry can well be accepted but the necessity for despotism is extremely obscure, using 'despotism' in the standard rather vague way simply to denote authoritarian, non-democratic forms of rule. Marx gives no logical foundation for this point, which really is no more than an assertion. It is not however one of Marx's 'holiday pronouncements'. It is a point stressed at several places in *Capital*, as well as in the *Communist Manifesto*, commonly using the metaphor of the army. For example he argues that modern industry gives rise to 'a barrack discipline, which is elaborated into a complete system in the factory, and which fully develops the before mentioned labour of overlooking, thereby dividing the workpeople into operatives and overlookers, into private soldiers and sergeants of an industrial army' (Marx 1954, p. 399).

The concept of the despotism of the factory is closely linked to Marx's analysis of the transition from manufacture to modern industry, conceived of as the breaking up of skilled artisan tasks into their components and thus imposing a greater need for supervision and co-ordination. Even within this framework however it is not clear why the subordination should be despotic. Here again neither legally nor *de facto* does private possession give capitalist firms the unconstrained ability to use labour power in the way they wish. Legally they are constrained by Factory Acts, forms of labour contracts, etc., and of course non-legally by worker and trade union pressure.

Now 'practically' Marx recognizes this. In *Capital* (vol. i, Ch. x) for example Marx gives his well-known long account of the struggles in the nineteenth century over the Factory Acts. The workers' victory in this area is hardly consistent with the notion of an untrammelled despotism. Here there is one of those disparities which were noted at the beginning: Marx's work is not all of a piece. General theoretical positions are not necessarily consistent with political analysis.

Despite this disparity, the theory of despotism of capital continues to inform socialist discussions of the enterprise. For example the Brighton Labour Process Group (1977) argue the necessity for 'hierarchy' in production in a way theoretically compatible with Marx. The particular pertinence of this in this instance is to argue that 'semi-autonomous' work groups really alter nothing, they reflect only a changed technology of hierarchy and control rather than its displacement.[6] In such a way the BLPG set up a dichotomy between the bourgeois pretence that such work groups somehow usher in the realm of freedom and the Marxist understanding that really they alter nothing. The Marxist pole of this dichotomy functions then to make it impossible to conceive that changes such as autonomous work groups are anything but straightforwardly another face of an unchanging essence, the despotism of capital. This doesn't have to be demonstrated – it is a logical necessity. To oppose this conception need not be to endorse the bourgeois view, merely to argue for a 'space' for specific analysis of these work groups, their conditions and effects, rather than to offer simply a pre-judgement.

Many of the same points would be relevant to the attempt to deduce despotism from the nature of the enterprise as an entity producing commodities and surplus value. Combined with essentialist notions of legal status, the conception of the despotism of capital derived from the commodity-producing character of the capitalist enterprise, has tended to produce a simple derivative form of analysis in which the non-legal aspects of organization of the enterprise (e.g. forms of division of labour, managerial practices) are simply derived from the profit-making character of the enterprise. Such notions, it can be argued, generate a very simplistic and unhelpful conception of the enterprise. Whilst enterprises under capitalism are constrained to reproduce themselves financially ('have a positive cash flow'), this can be done in an enormous variety of ways (witness the variety of ways it *is* achieved in different capitalist countries) and involves no necessary form of organization (witness the struggles and changes in forms of organization within capitalist countries). The argument that all capitalist enterprises are essentially alike can only be shown tautologically – they are all alike *because* they are capitalist.

The argument that the demands of commodity production and the need to make a profit structure the enterprise because they generate a conflict of interest between capitalist and workers appears equally problematic. First, to talk of a general conflict of interest which is simply played out within the enterprise is unhelpful. The enterprise *constructs* the agents who are going to struggle in the enterprise and is not simply a stage upon which workers and capitalists act out a drama directed from elsewhere. These struggles are over particular questions – wages, conditions, control – which cannot be analysed simply as effects of a general conflict of interest. But even if the concept of a general conflict were accepted there is no good reason why this should lead to 'despotism'. Depending on the practices of all the agents within the enterprise, conflicts may be resolved in a range of ways, and indeed it is difficult to conceive what the absolute subordination of one interest to another would appear like if this is what despotism is taken to suggest.

Overall the argument is that neither from the need for co-ordinating production nor from the commodity character of production can one derive a despotism. This is not of course to deny the often tyrannical practices which can exist in enterprises – because of the evasion of laws, the weakness of trade unionism, the state of the labour market, etc. – but it is to argue that such practices cannot be derived from a notion of capitalist relations of production in the broad sense of commodity production determined by profit calculation in which labour power is also a commodity.

The concept of fetishism and the arguments derived from it have clear implications for the analysis of enterprise calculation.[7] As already noted, for Marx the form of calculation engaged in by enterprises is both the effect of capitalist relations of production and a condition for their survival. The first point means that the form of calculation must be conceived of as invariant for as long as capitalism survives. Capitalists are locked into certain positions in the relations of production which gives them the 'experience' or 'vision' which generates certain necessary forms of calculation. The problem with this is that it makes impossible the variety of calculations of profit which actually exist in capitalist countries (see G. Thompson 1978) or it makes these differences merely different representations of an underlying similarity. Once this diversity is given any weight then a simple derivation from capitalist relations of production becomes impossible – calculations of profit, etc. cannot be seen simply as effects of the position capitalists occupy in the relations of production, effects of the way in which the economy 'appears' to them.

Similarly for the second pole of the argument, that a definite form of calculation is a necessary condition for the reproduction of the enterprise, cannot be sustained. A whole variety of calculations manage to sustain capitalist enterprises. The two simple forms of profit calculations ascribed by Marx to capitalists, those relating to cost prices of production, which he puts most emphasis on, or total capital (Reati 1980) employed by no means exhaust the forms of profit calculation employed in a capitalist economy. Not only are there different bases (e.g. equity outstanding) on which to calculate profit but these bases themselves are extremely problematic – for example what is to count as 'capital' is of course open to a great deal of debate. If Marx's presumption of the reflective nature of forms of calculation is discarded then a whole range of arguments are possible about the conditions and effects of *various* forms of calculation. Thus G. Thompson (1978) has shown the variety of forms of profit calculations and how they have effects upon, *inter alia*, taxation, wage bargaining and the distribution of investment. This means that forms of calculation need not be conceived of as unitary nor as functional to capitalism but as variable and open to challenge and for socialist ideology *worthy* of challenge because they have significant implications for the economy. As with arguments about hierarchy, the deconstruction of Marx's notions of calculation, far from making a relapse into bourgeois forms of analysis, can broaden the front of socialist attack on capitalist practices.

It may be argued against this that capitalist relations of production (commodity production on the basis of calculation of profits; wage labour) require some necessary forms of accounting and therefore subvert this disparity of forms. Certainly it can be accepted that profit calculations are inescapable consequences of capitalism defined as production determined by profit criteria. The point is that such calculations have no simple 'cause' and therefore no unitary effects. The word profits does not 'represent' a single underlying entity, it is not a 'sign' of something else. It is a concept with a meaning constructed by the particular discourse of which it is a part.

In addition to the above points the question of calculation raises questions of competence. If forms of calculation are *not* conceived of as misleading phenomenal forms, which once dissipated will make reality immediately visible (which is a possible though not in-escapable consequence of Marx's argument), then there can never be a day when there will be a 'transparent' form of calculation derived from the visible essence of the production process. If calculation by contrast is an object of never-resolved (because never resolvable) argument then there must be competence to be learned in order to argue about different forms of calculation and their effects. Arguments about workers' control must then involve questions about the learning of such competences, otherwise effective control will remain a utopian objective.

Marx's conception of the production process in terms of a *labour* process can, like the other concepts discussed, be analysed in a number of ways. One can question its logical foundations in either the labour theory of value (Cutler *et al.* 1977, Pt I) or in an anthropological conception of labour (Cutler 1978). These arguments in their general form will not be repeated here. But the privileging of labour has clear consequences for the analysis of production. For example, if the characteristics of labour are the key to production processes then managerial practices must be conceived as above all operating on these characteristics. Managers are then seen as 'monomaniacs' – all enterprise strategies are subordinated to the strategy aimed 'against' labour.

This view can be produced in a number of ways. For example managers can be conceived as calculating to maximize the separation of the labour of 'conception' and 'execution' because of its effects on value creation (Braverman 1974, pp. 113–14). This however is strictly illogical in Marx's terms because as we have seen for him capitalists necessarily calculate in non-value (money) terms. Alternatively managers can be seen as calculating directly to separate 'conception' and 'execution' in order to minimize labour's capacity to resist. This however is a paradoxical argument because it commonly (e.g. Braverman, Ch. 6) goes along with the notion that because this separation will offend the human essence it will *cause* recalcitrance on the part of labour. From this latter position it would seem just as logical to argue that managers will calculate to combine labours of 'conception' and 'execution' in order to limit recalcitrance.

Braverman is placing a central stress on capitalist calculation as being a calculation on labour's attributes and so rather distorts and over-simplifies Marx's own arguments. From Braverman one gains the impression that like everything else machinery is introduced solely to 'de-skill' the workforce. Marx himself (1954, p. 351) stresses that 'like every other increase in the productiveness of labour, machinery is intended to cheapen commodities'. Within this general objective the introduction of machinery may be speeded up to displace a skilled 'cunning workman' (p. 407) by an unskilled worker, but this cannot on Marx's warrant be constructed into a general tendency of capitalism (see also note 1 to this chapter).

Yet it is partly on the basis of the elaboration of such a tendency that Taylorism can play the extraordinary central role it does in Marxist analyses of management – because Taylorism is seen as above all operating on the characteristics of labour. Thus for Braverman[8] (p. 86), 'It is impossible to overestimate the importance of the scientific management movement in the shaping of the modern corporation' because Taylorism is the 'explicit verbalisation of the capitalist mode of production'. Leaving aside the knotty question of how a mode of production verbalizes itself, this centrality given to Taylorism raises a series of problems. Firstly it seems clear that Taylorism was not directed mainly at the 'labour problem' when introduced in the USA but was seen as a 'comprehensive answer to the problems of factory co-ordination, a refinement and expansion of systematic management' (Nelson 1974, p. 480). Secondly Taylorism was only one of a spectrum of managerial innovations introduced towards the end of the nineteenth century and the beginning of the twentieth – e.g. personnel administration and management accounting. Marxist analyses of these tend to present them as part of an orchestrated set, structured around the labour problem (e.g. Parker 1975) but the orchestration is assumed, again because of the assumed centrality of the 'labour problem' (see Nelson and Campbell 1972).

More generally the problems of Marxist accounts of Taylorism open up the whole notion of labour being conceived in terms of the dichotomies conception/execution or mental/manual. Such dichotomies must subvert any helpful analysis of the division of labour because they set up an unsustainable polarity. No labour can be either

24

wholly mental or wholly manual, or wholly of conception or execution.

This point is recognized by the Brighton Group. They rightly stress that 'all human labour involves both mind and body. Manual labour involves perception and thought. . . . Equally, all mental labour involves bodily activity' (p. 17). They argue that the mental/manual distinction should be formulated as

> the division between those who produce or apply scientific knowledge in the design of production systems and in day-to-day problem solving involved in the operation of the system, and those whose relationship with the production system is calculated, standardised and specified in advance by capital in the interests of producing an output which is known with precision in advance. (p. 17)

This reformulation seems not to evade the problems of the cruder dichotomy it is aimed to displace. Firstly because the distinction seems problematic in the sense that it tries to establish differences which seem far from hard and fast. Secondly it fails to specify the mechanisms whereby capitalism maintains this division, which they argue is 'immanent in the capitalist labour process' (p. 17). Finally the conception once again rests on an unambiguous notion of who controls production – in this case a control maintained by capital's monopoly of the knowledge and power over the design of production systems. The question of 'control' of production is taken up in Chapter 7.

The general argument here is that the conception of the 'labour process' as central to the analysis of the capitalist enterprise is unhelpful because it generates functionalist accounts of management – management fulfils functions required for the realization of the tendencies of capitalism in relation to labour. Such conceptions cannot then cope with the diversity of management forms. To paraphrase Marx, the bourgeoisie are 'constantly revolutionising the means of management', and it is no help in analysing these changing means to reduce them all to a functional unity. The focus on the labour process has also been one reason why Marxist accounts of management appear so one-dimensional. Problems which govern the activities of most managers – marketing, cash flow, supply of components, quality control, etc. – are striking by their absence because they are not readily assimilable to the assumed over-arching question of the management of labour.

One other general problem with the conception of production in terms of a labour process should be identified. At the beginning of this chapter it was argued that at its most general Marx's notion of enterprise conceives of it as an 'aliquot part' of the total social capital. This suggests the enterprise is a financial entity, united by its control over a proportion of the total social capital. The discussion of company law implies the notion of the company as a *legal entity*, though this may not define a very different boundary from the financial. But the focus on the labour process seems to lead to the concept of 'the factory', that is an entity in which there is some kind of unified direction of a labour process. This clearly implies a different kind of enterprise from those implied in the financial and legal definitions. Thus there is a tension in Marx's account between what might be called a theory of factory organization *à la* Babbage (1835) and Ure (1834) (because of the centrality of the labour process) and a theory of the distribution of capital (because of the conception of individual capitals as subject to mode-of-production-wide laws of motion). This kind of tension in the definition of the enterprise is a problem common to all accounts of the capitalist enterprise, and is addressed at some length in the concluding chapter to this book.

III

To Marx's conception of homogeneous, despotic enterprises, with given forms of calculation and analysed best in terms of a labour process, has been counterposed a notion of the enterprise which denotes a set of heterogeneous practices which have mutual inter-dependence (e.g. company law requires certain forms of profit calculation) but no given unity, which have varying conditions of existence and tend towards no one particular end. Conceived in this way the enterprise can be seen as a site for a multiplicity of interventions by socialists, because all the different practices of the enterprise can be challenged in some degree separately. By contrast the orthodox Marxist position tends to imply that because the enterprise has an 'essential' character one either fights that essence (however conceived) or engages in what must be seen as necessarily unimportant battles because they concern only peripheral issues.

NOTES

1 This produces the paradoxical implication that in so far as the socialist factory is based on co-operative labour it too will be despotic – see Engels (1892).
2 Marx's argument on this is at points ambiguous; this is his most consistent formulation.
3 As Cutler (1978) points out, the notion of 'de-skilling' for Marx relates to the artisan mode of production and therefore it cannot simply be 'applied to capitalism'.
4 This of course partly accounts for the interminable debates about the tendency of the rate of profit to fall.
5 For a more detail discussion of Marxism and company law see Hirst (1979a).
6 Gorz (1978) also endorses this argument: 'As a functionary of capital, he [the capitalist] must retain absolute despotic power over the workplace' (p. 56).
7 For a summary of general problems of festishism as a theory of ideology see for example Rose (1977).
8 Braverman's argument is concentrated on here because of its prominence in recent discussions. Critiques of his work (e.g. Elger 1979) do not focus on this central role of Taylorism even if they do want to relate it to a 'crisis of accumulation'.

CHAPTER TWO

Marxist analysis: examples and problems

In this chapter the arguments of modern British Marxism about the capitalist enterprise are explored using two extended examples. These examples are those of co-operatives and 'industrial democracy' in the particular sense of worker directors on the boards of directors of capitalist enterprises. Discussion of these two examples by British Marxism is used as a way of exploring the general lines of argument that this Marxism uses in attempting to come to terms with the capitalist enterprise.

Clearly there is a problem in talking about British or indeed any other 'Marxism'. Marxism has become such a dispersed, heterogeneous – not to say chaotic – collection of doctrines that any attempt to define a true Marxism must quickly either become dogmatic or decline into vacuity by defining Marxism so broadly that practically no one could not be a Marxist. Such problems cannot always be easily resolved by appealing to the works of Marx and Engels as these themselves are far from being a coherent and homogeneous canon. However, in this case I think that with all the qualifications that should be entered about for example not seeing political arguments as simply theories 'made fresh', British Marxism has in broad terms been faithful to the Marxism of Marx in its discussion of co-operatives and industrial democracy. I have attempted to show this by beginning the discussion with some excerpts from Marx. These relate to co-operatives, but as will be argued below some at least of the positions taken up by Marx have been used in recent discussions of both co-operatives and industrial democracy.[1]

I

As in so many areas Marx did not write an extended theoretical account of co-operatives, but rather his positions were part of on-going political arguments. A fairly systematic statement was made in an article under the name of Ernest Jones, but which Marx said 'had been written in the main points under my direction and in part even with my close participation' (Marx and Engels 1979, p. 686 n. 360).[2]

The main thrust of the article (Marx and Engels 1979, pp. 573–81) is first that the capacity of co-operative producers and distributors to compete with capitalists is weak indeed so that there is 'an inequality that might almost deter from the attempt' (p. 575). This point is applied to producer co-operatives, and Jones argued that workers' co-operatives would always have to charge higher prices than competing capitalists, especially because of 'the constantly developed power of machinery, which he can always command the readiest' (p. 577). Jones then argues that co-operative production is dependent on the growth of demand, which in turn depends on the prosperity of the working class. Thus he argues that to achieve this demand, 'You want some third power to ensure success. In fine, you want political power to reconstruct the bases of society' (p. 577).

The tendency for co-operatives to degenerate into what were effectively profit-making joint stock companies is stressed. From this is drawn the conclusion that what is needed is to 'nationalise co-operation' so that every local association is the branch of a national one with profits pooled to finance the expansion of the movement. Without this co-operatives will either fail or succeed only by becoming like their capitalist competitors. (There is a second article in this collection on co-operatives but relating only to distributive types.)

Later, in his inaugural address to the International Working Men's Association, Marx talked about co-operatives in a way which is worth quoting in full (Marx 1974, pp. 79–80).

But there was [in 1848] in store a still greater victory of the political economy of labour over the political economy of property. We speak of the co-operative movement, especially the co-operative factories raised by the unassisted efforts of a few bold 'hands'. The value of these great social experiments cannot be overrated. By deed, instead of by argument, they have shown that production on a large scale, and in accord with the behests of modern science, may

29

be carried on without the existence of a class of masters employing a class of hands; that to bear fruit, the means of labour need not be monopolised as a means of dominion over, and of extortion against, the labouring man himself; and that, like slave labour, the serf labour, hired labour is but a transitory and inferior form, destined to disappear before associated labour plying its toil with a willing hand, a ready mind, and a joyous heart. In England, the seeds of the co-operative system were sown by Robert Owen; the working men's experiments, tried on the Continent, were, in fact, the practical upshot of the theories, not invented, but loudly pro-claimed, in 1848.

At the same time, the experience of the period from 1848 to 1864 has proved beyond doubt that, however excellent in principle, and however useful in practice, co-operative labour, if kept within the narrow circle of the casual efforts of private workmen, will never be able to arrest the growth in geometrical progression of monopoly, to free the masses, nor even to perceptibly lighten the burden of their miseries. It is perhaps for this very reason that plausible noblemen, philanthropic middle-class spouters, and even keen political economists, have all at once turned nauseously com-plimentary to the very co-operative labour system they had vainly tried to nip in the bud by deriding it as the utopia of the dreamer, or stigmatising it as the sacrilege of the socialist. To save the industrious masses, co-operative labour ought to be developed to national dimensions, and, consequently, to be fostered by national means. Yet the lords of land and the lords of capital will always use their political privileges for the defence and perpetuation of their economical monopolies. So far from promoting, they will continue to lay every possible impediment in the way of the emancipation of labour. Remember the sneer with which, last session, Lord Palmerston put down the advocates of the Irish Tenants' Right Bill. The House of Commons, cried he, is a house of landed proprietors. To conquer political power has therefore become the great duty of the working classes.

Finally in his instructions for delegates to the Geneva Congress of the IWMA Marx wrote (1974, p. 90):

(a) We acknowledge the co-operative movement as one of the transforming forces of the present society based upon class antagonism. Its great merit is to practically show, that the present pauperising and despotic system of the subordination of labour to capital can be superseded by the republican and beneficient system of the association of free and equal producers.

(b) Restricted, however, to the dwarfish forms into which individual wage slaves can elaborate it by their private efforts, the co-operative system will never transform capitalistic society. To convert social production into one large and harmonious system of free and co-operative labour, general social changes are wanted, changes of the general conditions of society, never to be realised short of the transfer of the organised forces of society, viz., the state power, from capitalists and landlords to the producers themselves.

In the 1970s the question of co-operatives was raised for socialists particularly by the advent of the co-operatives of Meriden, Kirkby Manufacturing and Engineering and the *Scottish Daily News*, each of which emerged from a situation of threatened redundancies. (For accounts of these see Coates 1976; Oakeshott 1978; on Kirkby, Eccles 1981.) The general tenor of Marxist responses has been similar, though with varying degrees of qualification and sophistication in the argument. Clarke (1977, p. 372) argued that 'in the absence of a general transformation of production relations, workers in isolated co-operatives remain at the mercy of market forces and government controls which destroy the possibility of substantial internal reform'. These production relations impose themselves by the necessity for the co-operative to make profits to survive. 'In Britain one of the saddest things we have seen in the Labour movement in recent years is the struggle of workers at the S.D.N. and at Triumph Meriden to take over unprofitable concerns and try to run them better than the bosses did. They are forced to run them for profit and the sacrifices have been tragic' (Cliff and Peterson 1976, p. 13). Because of the necessity of making profits the internal character of the firm is fixed:

> The running of a newspaper, or any other enterprise, along commercial lines requires that commercial considerations come first. Workers management sounds attractive but that management would face the same problems as the Beaverbrook management (at SDN).
>
> It would have to try and solve them by trimming the workforce, by jacking up productivity, by pushing 'flexibility' and generally undermining the conditions that union action has achieved in the industry.

31

. . . You cannot build islands of socialism in a sea of capitalism. (*Socialist Worker* 1974)

A similar point can be expressed in more clearly Marxist language:

Capitalist relations of production consist not only of intra enterprise relations (capitalists/managers: workers) but also of inter enterprise relations (that is relations between private capitals which are market regulated and unplanned). Because of this it is difficult, for example, for workers co-operatives to break away from capitalist principles of organisation (hierarchy, wage differentials, minimisation of wage costs, etc.). This is obvious enough perhaps in the case of the sole co-operative that seeks to stay afloat on the capitalist sea. But the same tendencies will assert themselves even if we consider the notional case of a society in which workers have appropriated all enterprises and seek to run them democratically, and on the basis of equality – unless, that is, they have had the foresight to abolish the commodity relations which formerly entangled these enterprises. (Nichols 1980, p. 25)

If the firm has problems these problems are irresolvable within capitalism: 'the problems of Triumph are not due to the whims of the bosses but the hard logic of the capitalist system' (Parker 1975, p. 28). Impelled in this way by the logic of the system, by profit making, co-operatives can go only two ways:

'There have been many examples of workers co-operatives that went wrong: there have been some that have "succeeded" – in capitalist terms that is! All that they have succeeded in, however, has been to transform themselves into profitable capitalist enterprises, operating in the same way as other capitalist firms' (Mandel 1975, p. 8). The negative implications of these lines of argument are explicit. Sparks (1974, p. 18) assesses Meriden as follows: 'a manager (on £8,000 a year) straight from Jaguar Boardroom; a drastically reduced workforce; an amazing increase in productivity; a maximum wage well below what they could get elsewhere in Coventry; the Department of Trade and Industry as a nanny to monitor every move they made'. Logically, from such an assessment stems the conclusion: 'We do not advocate it (i.e. co-operatives) under capitalism. Specifically in the case of closures we call for nationalisation, not state aid to co-operative enterprises' (*International Socialism* 1974, p. 25).

I have quoted from a range of Marxist sources, but the fundamentals of the argument are remarkably similar in each case. These fundamentals may be expressed in three propositions.

1 Profit maximization, central to the operations of a capitalist economy, provides a clear-cut criterion on firms as to their success or failure. This measure in turn regulates the flow of investment from elsewhere in the economy and so governs the survival or otherwise of the firm. (The operation of the much vaunted 'law of value' often amounts in effect to no more than this.)
2 Co-operatives (or indeed any other form of enterprise) if they are to survive in a profit-making economy will have to adopt the management practices of capitalist firms, imposed by profit-maximization, or go out of business.
3 Thus 1 and 2 imply that co-operatives as effective alternatives to capitalist enterprises cannot exist without an overthrow of the entire capitalist system, without the seizure of state power by the workers.

The first proposition partly rests on the notion of profit maximization as (in principle) an unambiguous objective for the firm to pursue. Only if this is the case would it seem possible for the outcome of this maximization in terms of profits *realized* to act as a regulator of investment flows and ultimately the survival or otherwise of enterprises.

The conception of an unambiguous notion of profit is a difficult one to defend. As recent debates over inflation accounting have made clear, profit as an accounting term is extremely ambiguous and open to a large number of definitions – this is clearly brought out by Sandilands (1975, para. 77):

> Many different views may be taken of the extent to which gains of all kinds may be regarded as profit for the year. . . . The extent to which a given amount of total gain is regarded as profit may vary between nil and 100 per cent, depending on the point of view of the individual or company involved and on the conventions of accounting system adopted. (see also G. Thompson 1978).

This is not of course to imply that each and every enterprise defines profits according to its own whims. Profit calculations in the UK operate within a framework laid down mainly by the accounting profession (in other countries accounting standards are the subject of legal regulation).[3] But this framework is a loose one, allowing for a considerable range of variation in firms' calculations. This point is accepted by some supporters of capitalism who nevertheless want to argue that the economy operates 'as if' firms profit maximized. Firms' habits and chance calculations are seen as having effects *as if* based on clear-cut profit maximization (Friedman 1953). Winter (1964) has effectively demolished such arguments by showing first that 'chance' and 'habit' cannot guarantee maximizing behaviour in *all* conditions. Secondly he shows that even if in one situation random behaviour does lead to profit maximization and does lead to the firm's expansion, there is no good reason why this should operate systematically so that high profit firms consistently expand and poor profit performers consistently decline.

The implication of this argument is that profit levels cannot act as a simple regulator of the growth or decline of firms. This point is recognized by investing institutions in the economy, who do not treat announced profit levels as a major criterion for investing in enterprises. Rather such investment criteria involve a diverse set of calculations including *inter alia* capital structure, future cash flow, character of the management, industrial relations, product range, etc. These have no simple correlation with a mythical unambiguous notion of profit.

The objective of this line of argument is not to suggest that profit maximization at one level of analysis is not a helpful way of conceiving the operations of a capitalist firm. Though in Chapter 7 it is argued that 'financial reproduction' is a more useful concept in many contexts, the assumption of profit maximization in certain arguments is a useful analytical device. But the important point, even assuming 'profit maximization', is that pursuit of such an objective is a much looser rein on the operations of any particular firm than is commonly implied, and as is strongly implied by many (including the Marxist) critics of co-operatives cited above.

Secondly, even if we picture all firms as trying to maximize their profit levels there is no reason to suppose this leads to any one conclusion as to how this maximization is to be achieved. Such an end does not imply any necessary means. Profit maximization by the firm can helpfully be compared with a military general attempting to use an army to win a battle. In both cases there is a clear objective but in neither case does this objective imply any one solution. Firms like generals have *strategies*, a term which itself implies room for manoeuvre, room for diverse calculations, diverse practices to be brought to bear on the objective.

Of course neither army nor firm begin *ex nihilo*. Both begin with an already existing array of forces which constrains their strategy. Equally, their choice of strategy is not just a random process. The army's strategy will be conditioned by the current 'state of the art' as propagated by military manuals, military academies, the current generation of generals, etc. In the same way the management of the firm will be conditioned by current managerial ideologies as reflected in management organizations, management journals, business schools and the informal consensus of management.

The diversity of managerial strategies pursued by capitalist firms is apparent. Some have been very 'liberal', some very 'authoritarian' in their industrial relations policies. Some have stressed sales maximization and small profits per item sold, some large profits on small quantities. Some have focused on technological developments as the way to long-run profits while others have focused on selling techniques as the way to success. The variations can be almost infinitely multiplied. None of them has been unambiguously successful or unsuccessful in maximizing profits – profit maximizing is an extremely speculative business rather than an objective with simple logical implications for the way to run a firm.

The relevance of these points for the discussion of co-operatives should be clear. Whilst co-operatives operating in a predominantly capitalist economy are hemmed in by, for example, the need to get finance, or the need to sell their goods at prices which will provide a positive cash flow, they are not so tightly hemmed in as the common Marxist argument suggests. They have to have a concern for financial survival but this does not mean that to successfully achieve this there is only one way, ' the capitalist way'. If this were the case how could the diversity of the capitalist firm's practice be explained other than as irrationality, with discussion of the firm an extended essay on psychopathology? Like the capitalist firm, the co-operative is constrained (and in some respects more severely – see below) but there are still strategic possibilities – possibilities of diverse managerial practices compatible with financial survival.

The implication of the existence of these 'strategic possibilities' is that co-operatives which do have different forms of organization to the generality of capitalist enterprises *can* survive under capitalist conditions. That is, there is no need to set up the argument in terms of total sets of social relations: one (capitalism) which forbids co-operative success, another (socialism) which permits it. Another way of putting this is to argue that the constraints that co-operatives suffer under can be lessened without any revolutionary change in social relations. (I do not here criticize the notion of state power which is crucial to the Marxist argument. This has been done extensively elsewhere; see, for a powerful recent example, Minson (1980), but its analogue in the notion of *control* of the firm is discussed in Chapter 7.)

Undoubtedly the most important constraint facing most co-operatives is that of finance (Thornley 1981, Ch. 3) and such constraints are well illustrated in the cases of the co-operatives, at Meriden, SDN and Kirkby. All three were particularly hard pressed in this regard because they originated from firms which were already in financial difficulties. In each case temporary survival was achieved only by state funding, itself the result of a highly particular struggle within the government and state bodies (see especially Eccles 1981).

Certain kinds of financing, such as that from banks and pension funds, might be available to co-operatives which were not so clearly encumbered by past financial difficulties as the three examples above. However the problem is of course that this finance would probably be granted under restrictive conditions which would go beyond simply asking for a certain rate of return on the money lent. Indeed this is a major way that managerial norms are imposed on firms, by being the condition of financing. This happened to Meriden where the lenders (in this case another company, GEC) gave financial help on condition of changes in management in the co-operative.

Given that other forms of finance would be ruled out by the objectives of the co-operative (for example the issue of voting shares to people outside the enterprise)[4] then access to funding without objectionable strings attached is a vital problem. However there is no reason to suppose that the creation of a specific financial institution aimed at aiding co-operatives, imposing financial constraints on co-operatives but also encouraging alternative forms of organization, is pie in the sky this side of the socialist millennium. Given the diversity of political support for co-operatives, albeit for different reasons (see Tomlinson 1980a), this would not seem an impossible task for socialists to set themselves.[5] There would seem to be considerable space in Britain for the creation of new kinds of financial institution, given that compared with other capitalist countries this sector in Britain is very homogeneous and little regulated by state agencies.[6]

A second major problem of co-operatives is that of management. Here two arguments that are commonly confused in the discussion need to be separated out. One is the question of management 'functions' – the jobs of co-ordinating production, planning invest- ment and output levels, organizing sales of the product, etc. These functions would seem to be inescapable in any kind of modern enterprise – they cannot be avoided. This is not to say that everything management currently does has to be done since many of their activities are clearly highly dependent on particular features of capitalist firms – the endemic conflict between workers and man- agers, the commitment to managerial rights, etc. But some man- agerial functions are not like this, they will always have to be carried out.

The second question is that of who is to carry out these unavoidable managerial functions. Often it is implied that if the necessity of management is once conceded then its current form of activity has to be defended. This is definitely not the case. Firstly of course, as has been stressed above, management is subject to fashions and trends which should encourage scepticism about claims that its current ways of operating should be treated as the only rational ways. More importantly there is the question of *who* is to carry out managerial functions – do they have to be the preserve of a separate (and privileged) part of the workforce. Here it can be argued that there is a great deal of scope for 'de-professionalizing' management – parcelling out many of its current functions amongst the workforce, and so breaking down the division of labour between the manager and the managed. Such a view is not utopian if it is coupled with a clear notion that the competences and abilities to perform managerial functions do not fall from the sky – they have to be learnt. No one automatically has these capacities, be they workers or professional managers. So any attack on the current division of managerial functions must be coupled with a realistic assessment of how abilities are learnt and the obstacles that face such learning.

Thus when it is argued that co-operatives can only survive with 'professional management' a coherent response is not to argue that management is only necessary in capitalist firms and can be made to disappear if the workers themselves run the enterprise. Such a position precisely conflates a sociological category ('persons who manage') with a function. But equally it is implausible to argue that the current way management works, and the personnel who do the managing, was handed down on tablets of stone and that any attack on it will result in abject failure. (This is broadly the position of

Oakeshott (1978).) Management is necessary as a function but *how* it is done is open to a great deal of change and reconstruction.

Once the conceptual separation of (some) management functions from particular personnel is effected then again the possibility of change without socialist revolution is apparent. Reforms would be required in diverse areas such as education, in industrial training and in such areas as job design, etc. Equally, socialists would have to argue strongly against those within and without the labour movement who defend the existing division of labour in the enterprise as sanctioned by the natural order or by the necessities of efficiency. The crucial point in the current context is that such reforms are possible *within* capitalist social relations as normally defined, i.e. predominantly private ownership of the means of production.

All three of the propositions with which I have characterized recent British Marxism's response to the co-operative experiments of the 1970s seem heavily flawed. They imply a set of social relations with very little space for manoeuvre for the enterprise and thus by extension that only a complete displacement of those social relations will open up such a 'space'. Against this it is suggested that enterprises operating in a capitalist economy are constrained, but not to the degree which makes any divergence from current capitalist norms impossible. The constraints are highly specific and amenable to reform (albeit contested) within the continued existence of capitalist social relations. The nature of these constraints is brought out very clearly in Eccles's (1981) discussion of the Kirkby co-operative and Berman's (1967) discussion of the co-operative plywood companies in the American North West.

II

In the mid-1970s another challenge to the existing form of capitalist enterprise in Britain materialized under the sign of industrial democracy. This concept, of course, covers an enormous range of heterogeneous positions, ranging from the most conservative kind of managerial 'consultation' with the workforce to workers' control. But the major crystallization of this challenge in Britain at least took a highly specific form – the proposal for worker directors put forward by the Bullock Committee (Bullock 1977). It was around these proposals that much of the socialist argument took place, and it is these arguments that the second half of this chapter discusses. This does not involve, it should be stressed, a defence of Bullock proposals *per se*; clearly these had severe weaknesses, many of them already diagnosed in relation to previous European systems of industrial democracy by Batstone and Davies (1976). The concern here is with the analytical framework that Marxist and other socialists brought to bear on the issue.

One argument that has been common in the debate, but which deserves only a mention in passing, is that concerning the intentions of those who put forward industrial democracy proposals, such as Bullock. A common theme is that industrial democracy proposals have been put forward by management as a way of not increasing workers' power but of channelling existing power into 'safer' channels. This is argued at length and in a historical context by Ramsay (1977) and in Nichols (1980). Ramsay argues that worker participation schemes have emerged not from a desire to 'humanize' capitalism but when management felt under challenge. 'Participation is thus best understood as a means of attempting to secure labour's compliance' (Ramsay 1977, p. 496; see also e.g. Clarke 1977). This point of course can be readily accepted (at least for the purposes of this argument) without any implication that this involves accepting any necessary outcome for such proposals. Any policy emanating from management can be seen as attempting to further their position – but managements do not thereby guarantee themselves success. Thus whilst an exposé of managerial motives in putting forward participatory and industrial democracy proposals may carry some political force it clearly cannot function as an argument for or against such proposals unless omniscience is granted to management. Outcomes are not determined by origins – in Marxist terms the class struggle decides who wins.

More important, indeed central, to the Left opposition to Bullock-style proposals is that argument which sees such proposals as a way of incorporating sections of the trade union movement into management roles in the firm. This theme is part of a broader one which sees 'the state' and capital as having a unified strategy towards trade unionism which oscillates between repression and incorporation (see especially Hyman 1975; a slightly different version is in Friedman 1977). The incorporation side, predominant recently, involves a variety of measures, especially incomes policies (see Tomlinson 1981a), as well as participatory/representative measures within the enterprise. In this framework it is argued that 'the general aim of management is to restrict conflict by containing it within joint regulatory institutions which blur the divergent interests of management and workers, erode the basis of independent workers organisation, and thereby inhibit the capacity of workers to take defensive action' (Clarke 1977, p. 356). In the same vein Ramelson (1975, p. 82) argued:

> We are totally opposed to the T.U.C. proposals contained in the Report of Industrial Democracy for worker directors in privately owned enterprises. . . . It is class collaborationist in character, dampens the class struggle, leads to corruption of workers representatives and is a deceptive sham of Industrial Democracy; its primary objective is to enmesh workers in running industry to provide maximum profit for the shareholders.

Similar positions are taken in, for example, Nichols and Beynon (1977), Friedman (1977), Coates (1980). The argument does *not* suggest that industrial democracy can successfully achieve this incorporation, because it always runs up against the limits of the incompatible interests of capital and labour – the class struggle may be suppressed but it will not go away. Thus Hugh Scanlon (quoted Clarke 1977, p. 356) said:

> there is a fundamental and, in finality, irreconcilable conflict between Capital and Labour. . . . 'Workers' participation' is, in my view, the greatest bulwark for preserving a free enterprise society. It does not seek to change, it seeks to perpetuate. It seeks to create the idea that there isn't a fundamental difference between us.

This of course is commonly linked to the idea of capitalists pursuing an unambiguous goal of profit maximization (as in the discussion of co-operatives). For example, 'In our opinion it is totally incompatible for workers to sit on the boards of private companies to deliberate on how best to maximise profit' (Labour Party 1976, p. 152).

Incorporation can never therefore be wholly successful, but nevertheless it has effects which are clearly deleterious. It means that the trade union 'bureaucracy' (which may be very broadly defined – see e.g. Hyman 1979) will become in effect a weapon of management by suppressing rank and file militancy. Trade union based board level representation will necessarily compromise the oppositional role of trade unions which reflects the true character of workers' interests as opposed to those of capital.

As with the argument above on co-operatives the Marxist argument about industrial democracy can be stated in the form of a few propositions without creating a straw man.

1 The interests of capitalist and workers' managements are given by (capitalist) social relations.
2 Within the firm these interests are reflected by on the one hand the drive for profit and on the other by rank and file militancy in opposition to management goals.
3 Therefore any weakening of this oppositional role will threaten the defence of working-class interests. This will occur through some sections of trade unions being incorporated to a greater or lesser extent into management objectives, thereby weakening the unions.

The first point is clearly a very broad one. It depends however on specifying interests in a very particular way. The notion of interests is obviously one widely used in all kinds of social scientific argument, and is not just confined to Marxists. Two major forms of the argument can be discerned.

The first is that which sees sets of social relations constructing interests which then 'continue' as long as those social relations exist. There is nothing necessarily Marxist in such a view. For example it may be based on analyses which see 'producers versus consumers', 'the rulers versus the ruled', etc. as the inescapable forms of interest construction (the Marxist version is of course capital versus labour). These are not the only interests but they are the fundamental ones, 'the control actors in the balance of class force in advanced capitalist societies' (Panitch 1980, p. 173).

The major alternative notion of interest is that which sees interests as *always* constructed, for example around a particular political programme, and never pre-given in social relations. This necessarily implies that interests may change independently of changes in social relations. (For an example of a political argument conducted in this way see Hirst (1981a).)

This distinction between conceptions of interest does not mean that any particular argument obviously falls into one or other of these categories – the two elements are often conflated. Thus for example an argument that a government's policies are in the 'interests of capital' can be looked at in either way. It can be a political calculation that in relation to specific objectives 'labour' is doing less well than 'capital' because of government activity. This may be an incorrect assessment

41

– a miscalculation. Such an assertion may equally stem from the notion that what the current government is doing is in the 'interests of capital' because what it is doing serves these always existent interests. That is, *if achieved*, government policies are necessarily favourable to capital – this is beyond political argument.

Again, these two positions may be run together in the sense that particular political calculations may be derived from the belief in general interests. But it is the relation between the general and the particular which is vital, the particular must in some sense be derivative of the general, must reflect the priority of the general in any particular argument.

The divergent interests of workers and capitalists for Marxism are not of course simply based on disputes over wages (though this may be the approach of some industrial relations argument). The worker/capitalist conflict is structured by the exploitative relation of production which involves not only wage payments but the whole pattern of capitalist domination of the workers' activities, both within and outside the factory and in the last analysis defines the whole society. This is why the worker/capitalist conflict is much more fundamental than say that between producer/consumer, which is merely ephemeral because it is not the *defining* conflict.

Because these interests are so deeply entrenched within (capitalist) society, arguments about interests are arguments about the survival of that society, that is the true interests of workers cannot be realized within capitalism but only through its overthrow and the creation of a new set of social relations which will reflect these interests (i.e. socialism).

The consequences from this kind of argument about interests for analysis of proposals for industrial democracy are clear. First the firm is seen as a 'stage' upon which already defined interests play out their inescapable roles. The enterprise is first and foremost an example, if a vital one, of something which is general to capitalist society. Industrial democracy is about the struggles of these already defined interests.

Secondly the discussion of any particular policy proposal such as industrial democracy must ultimately be linked to its ability to realize the true, objective, interests of the working class, that is socialism. Any other kind of analysis will mystify the underlying realities by focusing on the ephemeral rather than the vital forces.

One of the problems for Marxism, given this notion of 'true interest' of the working class, is how far is this to be seen as represented in existing organizations and practices. Of course in principle this interest would exist even if no one anywhere articulated it – it is inherent in social relations and is not the consequence of political argument. However, such a view is not usual amongst Marxists, and trade union activity is seen as at least in part an articulation of this interest. Of course there is a long history of Marxist critiques of trade unionism as representation of working-class interests (most famously Lenin's *What Is to Be Done?*) and Marxists have never given simple endorsements of trade union practices. But what, at least in Britain, has occurred recently is that, whilst falling short of being an adequate socialist practice, rank and file industrial militancy is seen as that which comes closest to representing the working-class interests (e.g. Panitch 1976; Hyman 1979). This then means that any attempt by unions to go against such militancy shows the extent to which they have indeed been incorporated into capitalism.

The conception of the enterprise as a stage upon which pre-given interests play out their assigned roles is similar in implication to the notion discussed above in relation to co-operatives, that enterprises cannot diverge from certain managerial practices if they are to survive. Both imply an incapacity in any particular enterprise to escape rigid lines laid down by capitalism 'as a whole'. In one version this coercion of the enterprise operates via the market, in the other via its insertion into a pre-given set of social relations. Alternatively one can see that such an approach must treat any industrial capital as merely an 'aliquot part' of the total social capital as Marx did.

British Marxism has thus provided a grid for the analysis of the enterprise which must treat any enterprise-specific argument as essentially beside the point. If one postulates no such 'representativeness' to enterprises then what is in the interest of any particular group of workers (or indeed capitalists) in an enterprise cannot be linked to a general discourse on capitalism/socialism because such 'representativeness' precisely implies general interests, that is interests common to all workers in all enterprises.

Of course it is impossible to refute (outside a naive positivism) the notion that general interests are at stake in each and every issue fought over in the enterprise. All that can be indicated are the implications of such an approach – in this instance the implications for the general way in which the enterprise is conceived. Also such an approach has political implications. It means that each and every struggle in the enterprise must be seen as either fundamentally unimportant or *in fact* reflecting on these general interests. This, it can be argued, sets the parameters for that common Marxist oscillation between disdain for particular trade union struggles and an attribution of disproportionate significance to each and every struggle.

The implication of this line of argument is that industrial democracy in the style of the Bullock proposals may have *no* significance for social relations in the sense of capitalism/socialism. The significance may only be in relation to interests conceived at a different level – the individual or groups of enterprises. To put it more concretely workers may well have an interest in persuading/forcing management into pursuing a particular product strategy to guarantee the viability of their enterprise. This clearly has no bearing of itself on capitalism/socialism but it can be denied that such an action would be in the interests of those proposing it. Any relation between such an action and the coming of socialism would appear entirely speculative.

This is not meant to imply that every enterprise is entirely separate from every other, its practices entirely unrelated to those of other enterprises. Of course industrial democracy implies changes in some areas which are common to enterprises – in company law for example. The point is that the generality of some enterprise practices does not homogenize their activities to such an extent that we 'can helpfully treat each as on a par with all others.

A final point is that treating industrial militancy as (imperfect) representation of true working-class interests has profound implications for the analysis of trade unionism in general and for industrial democracy in particular. Its general implication for the analysis of trade unionism is that it means that any strategic calculation about appropriate trade union policies is heavily weighted from the beginning in favour of rank and file militancy (whether over wages, job control or whatever). In Hyman's argument (1974, pp. 260–1) for example workers forcing out the 'frontier of control' are seen as always likely to be opposed by trade union officials because of their function as *negotiators* within the existing framework. What the argument ultimately depends on is a belief that the *experience* of the ordinary employee, his/her experience of 'the oppressive and exploitative relations of capitalist wage labour' will guarantee the appropriate socialist direction in the struggle. This experience gives a privileged access to the appropriate means to change the capitalist enterprise whereas the experience of the trade union official may lead him or her to a different *and wrong* assessment.

Once one questions the assumption that industrial militancy is a sign of the true interests of the working class then the role of trade union officials may be seen in a different light. Official trade union opposition to rank and file militancy, rather than being treated as always a sign of betrayal of true working-class interests, may (but only may) represent a (right or wrong) calculation about the appropriate strategy to achieve a particular objective. Whether an argument derives from a trade union official should not be seen as itself a major guide to the appropriateness of such an argument.

In relation to industrial democracy this means that there may well be conflicts between trade union officials who sit on the board and the current views of a workforce, but that this does not have to be interpreted as a sign of incorporation. It may simply reflect a different (right or wrong) calculation as to the correct strategy in a particular enterprise and situation.

This is *not* an argument for the autonomy of worker directors from workers. Of course the former should be elected, should be accountable and recallable. The point is rather that if interests are not treated as inherent in social relations but instead as the object of calculation, there is no simple/permanent division of positions into 'serving the workers' or 'serving capital' and no privilege to be accorded to particular social agents whose calculations (without the mechanisms being specified) are seen as representing their true interests.

Finally it is clear that proposals such as Bullock are deeply problematic for trade unionism. Trade unionism, especially in Britain, has traditionally defined its interests narrowly and defensively. Any attempt to break out from this role is (indeed has) created tensions and divisions. But there is no reason to suppose *a priori* that such a challenge to existing trade union practices is a bad thing, especially not on the basis of the analysis given by British Marxism (see also Hirst 1981b).

The position of British Marxism on the questions of co-operatives and industrial democracy has in broad and sometimes very crude terms reflected the kind of analysis of the enterprise given by Marx and criticized in Chapter 1. In particular, as I have tried to argue in this chapter, the *homogenization* of the enterprise, 'the capitalist enterprise', is implicated in both the analysis of 'market forces' given by

Marxism and its use of notions of interest (though this latter notion may reasonably be said to owe a great deal to a particular sociological account of Marxism as much as to classical Marxism). Also clear is that the notion of social relations as forming a totality is indeed central to the problems of Marxism (as argued by Cutler *et al.* 1977, 1978). Without this conception much of the Marxism outlined above would, strictly speaking, be unthinkable. For example the question of who has power over that totality would disappear, and the question of interests existing at the level of that totality likewise. The means by which one can talk about the enterprise without invoking such totalities is taken up in Chapter 7.

NOTES

1 It is not suggested here that British socialists' response to questions of co-operatives and industrial democracy are simply the 'practical' manifestation of adherence to Marxist theories. They are not *simply* anything, and equally hostility to co-operatives is, for example, strong in Fabian collectivism (see Chapter 3).

2 I am grateful to John MacInnes for pointing out the existence and importance of this article.

3 The legal requirements in British company law relating to profit declarations are minimal.

4 Though the non-voting share might be revived as a possible source of funding without 'control'.

5 Thornley (1981) argues that co-operatives will only be successful if allied with the 'mass organisations' of the Labour government. Against this I would suggest that the political *ambiguity* of co-operatives is something which creates a greater 'space' for pro-co-operative activity (including state funding) than would be the case if co-operatives were clearly in some sense 'socialist'.

   In other ways, however, Thornley's account, whilst using certain Marxist categories, escapes from most of the positions taken by British Marxism on co-operatives.

6 I have assumed that whatever arguments might be adduced for or against workers in a co-operative having a financial stake, this is not practicable as the sole means of financing of such enterprises.

CHAPTER THREE

The possibility of industrial democracy: Cole versus the Webbs

The programme of the guild socialists, above all the writings of G.D.H. Cole, represent probably the most sustained and coherent defence of 'industrial democracy' produced by British socialism. Guild socialist positions were in large measure directed against 'collectivism' for its opposition to such democracy, a doctrine represented above all by the Webbs. The arguments of and between these two factions[1] are the focus of this chapter, and are of interest because the arguments remain both theoretically and politically pertinent for modern socialist ideology. (There is no discussion of why guild socialism failed politically – on this see e.g. Pribecevic (1959); Hinton (1973).)

The significance of this debate was stressed by Wright (1979, especially Ch. IV) and some of its main features are outlined there. However, Wright links his discussion to questions of 'values' (p. 60) and questions of the meaning of democracy, whilst my concern is with the purely analytical character of the arguments produced and not with what those arguments may (allegedly) represent.

The basis of the Webbs' opposition to what they called 'associations of producers' as ruling elements in industry varies in its details and emphases throughout their work, and their Appendix VIII (1920b) represents at least a partial recantation. But my concern here is not with the question of whether the Webbs 'changed their minds' but the quality of the arguments which they presented, which are broadly similar throughout most of their work.

These arguments may be summarized as relating to (1) the inherent anti-consumer interests of producers, (2) the inherently hierarchical nature of modern industry and (3) the psychological impossibility of electoral structures in industry.

I

Many of these arguments are already present in Beatrice Webb's writings before her marriage (see Potter 1891/1930). She argued (p. 156) that

> it is a strangely distorted view of democracy to break a community into tiny self governing circles of producers, which by the very nature of their activities must fight each other to the death or combine to impose price and quality on the public. . . . For it is self-evident that all Associations of Producers . . . are directly opposed in their interests to the interest of the community.

This can only be offset if these groups of producers compete with each other, become thereby profit seekers and so undercut the 'spirit of combination'.

The same line of argument based on the 'exclusivity' of producers is developed in the Webbs' work (1920b, especially pp. 710–12), where such tendencies are seen as operating against the interests of both other groups of workers and especially the whole body of consumers and citizens. The argument is then that associations of producers always have clear-cut, pre-given interests which produce undesirable consequences. Associations of producers (based on trade unions) have no interest in lowering costs of production nor in responding to changes in demand. Above all such associations do not seek constantly to discover the best means of satisfying consumers' desires, and in this fail in comparison with directors of private firms or state and co-op officials (1920b, pp. 818–19).

Consequently producer democracy must be opposed above all because it infringes the sovereignty of consumers, their right to have their desires satisfied. Therefore the worker as a worker must accept that

> in the work that he does for the community in return for his subsistence he is, and must remain, a servant, subject to the instructions and directions of those whose desires he is helping to satisfy. As a Citizen-Elector jointly with his fellows, and as a

consumer to the extent of his demand, he is a master, determining, free from any superior, what shall be done. (ibid., p. 844)

A second major strand of argument against associations of producers is derived from a particular conception of modern industry. This industry is characterized as necessitating the 'subordination of the individual worker to masses of capital directed by expert intelligence' (Potter 1891, p. 168). Thus associations of producers *may* have been plausible had the craft stage of industry still been with us but is wholly inappropriate in relation to 'the novel facts of the new era of machinery'. This was something, Potter argued, grasped by Robert Owen who grappled with an industrial system 'necessitating a disciplined and highly organised army of workers, in different grades and varied capacities, all alike subordinated to the huge factory mechanism representing the labour of other bodies or generations of workers' (ibid., p. 120).[2]

The third major element in the Webbian argument was essentially a psychological one. This was that given the inescapable need for some kind of directing authority in industry, this role could not possibly be efficiently fulfilled if the manager/foreman were to be subject to electoral control by those supervised. For Potter such an arrangement is so self-evidently absurd that the only comment needed is an exclamation mark (Potter 1891, p. 153). 'Consider a railway managed on the system of the porters choosing the station master, the station master choosing the traffic superintendent, the whole body of employees choosing the board of directors!'

This point is reiterated by the Webbs (1914, p. 21), where human nature is said not to allow workers who employ a manager also to obey him, though it is accepted that this might be overcome by the spread of 'education and goodwill'. History is said to provide innumerable examples of this impossibility, that the relationship between director or manager and workers 'becomes hopelessly untenable if this director or manager is elected or dismissable by the very persons to whom he gives orders' (1920b, p. 713).

Of these three strands of argument it is the first which raises the most serious problems for socialist ideology and will be dealt with at most length here. The latter two are clearly important for socialist politics but the level of *argument* in the Webbs' and Cole's work is here much weaker than in comparison with the first so these arguments will be discussed much more briefly.

Cole's critique of the claims of collectivism starts from a critique of the notion of representation. This is vital because, he argues, the state's claim to control of industry in the collectivist scheme rests upon the idea of state sovereignty, and this claim of sovereignty in turn depends on claiming for the state the role of representative of the community (Cole 1919, Ch. V). Cole argues that this role is not only not fulfilled by the state but that it is impossible for any one organization to fulfil it. This impossibility arises from the incapacity of any institution, however democratic, to represent men's[3] wills in a general way. 'No man can represent another man, and no man's will can be treated as substitute for, or representative of, the wills of others' (1921, p. 103). Representation is not thereby impossible, but must be conceived as a representation of men for particular objects. This is seen as the form that most associations actually take.

> In the majority of associations, the nature of the relation is clear enough. The elected person – official, committee man, or delegate – makes no pretension of substituting his personality for those of his constituents, or of representing them except in relation to a quite narrow and clearly defined purpose or group of purposes which the association exists to fulfil. (ibid., p. 105).

This representation always distorts (p. 106) but this is not important as long as no detraction is made from the will of the individual.

For such a conception the state is not special because representative of men's wills, but only in being all-embracing because its particular purpose – the representation of men as consumers – is all-embracing in the sense of a functional purpose common to all. Even this position is later revised so that in the 1919 edition of *Self Government in Industry* Cole argues that there is no need for consumers to be represented by the state, but that 'the representation of men as "consumers, users and enjoyers" requires a multiplicity of associations dealing with the representation of different groups of purposes and interests' (p. 148 – see also Introduction to 1919 edition).

The implication of Cole's argument for the Webbs' position is quite clear. If the state cannot claim the right to represent the wills of men in general it must *at best* be seen as representing them only as consumers. If this is the case then this gives no right to control production because production is a different function, a sphere in which necessarily divergent interests exist as between different kinds of production and these should be represented through the guilds.

50

Thus guilds are 'a denial of the industrial sovereignty of the organised consumers' (Cole 1919, p. 133).

Against the Webbs' conception that men essentially have rights only as consumers Cole argues that they have divergent rights in divergent spheres and that none should be subordinated to any of the others. As Wright (1979, p. 57) stresses, the guild socialist argument 'was centrally concerned with the elaboration of the proper balance in each sphere and at every level between legitimate social interests, particularly the interests of producers and consumers'. The 1919 argument that the state does not represent even consumers is an important point in undercutting the homogenization of consumer interests accepted in the Webbs' position (and is important in relation to economic arguments which do precisely homogenize in this way). But the central point of criticism of collectivism remains unaltered – the state has no foundation for its claim to a right, based on representation, to control industry in the name of consumers.

Cole's criticism of the claims of collectivism is a criticism of the *right* of the state to claim sovereignty. This is a general criticism of all such claims, guild socialism being a consequence of applying this criticism in one particular sphere. In principle the same argument could be used wherever state sovereignty was claimed. This is one of the starting points of recent criticisms of the notion of parliamentary *sovereignty* (e.g. Hindess 1980), a notion which leads to the conception of the state as a unitary agency whose actions express the sovereign will (see also Hirst 1980).

Such criticisms however involve not only an attack on sovereignty as *right* but also sovereignty as *capacity*. That is parliament's claims to sovereignty can be undermined not only by means of attacks on the notion of parliament as representative, but also by means of attacks on its capacity effectively to subordinate all of the enormous number and variety of state agencies to its control. Such criticisms of sovereignty based on (in)capacity are relevant also to the question of industrial democracy.

The effective subordination of all production decisions to a central agency implies capacities on the part of that central agency which are simply impossible to conceive of in any substantial economy. This point was made long ago in anti-planning arguments, and one can accept the strength of such points without endorsing the general argument (see for example Hayek 1935). This problem is not capable of solution by computer: as Littlejohn (1979) argues, 'it has been calculated that the electronic representation of all the information required to centrally plan and manage the Soviet economy would require the use of more atoms than there are in the universe' (p. 224).

The political implications of such a view were spelt out many years ago, albeit in homely fashion, by Postgate (1920):

> if the proposal to run industry by Government Department is tyrannical and silly, the thought of Parliament controlling these departments is ridiculous. Parliament's control of the Ministry is at the best faint and vague. To imagine that six hundred-odd members, elected as they are now, are going in addition to protect the interests of democracy in the newly annexed soap works of Messrs. Jones in Huddersfield is singularly optimistic. The soap worker must do it. The battle of industry must be fought out in the industrial sphere.

This incapacity to control is not just a function of parliament's particular organization, but one general to any economy-wide agency of control.

The point here being made is that the extension of Cole's criticisms of sovereignty from rights to capacities extends the range of targets that can be hit. A sovereignty of rights underlies the Webbs' claims for the total subordination of production to the desires of consumers as expressed by the state. A sovereignty of capacities underlies the claims for *any kind of exhaustive* centralized economic planning, whether it be conceived of as based on consumer rights, the rights of the whole working class/nation or whatever.

In the face of such arguments the enterprise cannot be seen as simply a relaying point for decisions made elsewhere – it has variable but inescapable autonomy. The question of industrial democracy is not then simply a question of conflicts between 'general' and 'particular' interests where industrial democracy favours the latter. The enterprise can *never* operate simply as a 'technical' form necessary for realizing an objective imposed from outside, but the exigencies of its organization must always construct areas of conflict with external directive agencies. Arguments about industrial democracy can never then be sold on the basis of claims made by groups within the enterprise to represent the general will.

To put the general point more precisely and positively. If, as the Webbs argue, production is organized either at the behest of the producers or at the behest of consumers an untenable dichotomy is created. Either producers or consumers must determine what is produced – either one set of interests will triumph or the other one be sovereign of the other. Cole successfully challenges both poles of this dichotomy by challenging the sovereignty of rights of either group. As Wright stresses (1979, p. 52), Cole's argument was not one which refuted all claims of consumers or government, nor did it allege that workers represented the interests of the whole of society.

Cole's argument *is* an attack on consumer sovereignty, but a consumer sovereignty of particular kind – one where the state acts as an agent of representation of consumers, and as already noted, for Cole it is the bogus nature of this representation which undercuts the claims to sovereignty. The orthodox economists' notion of 'consumer sovereignty' is obviously different in some respects. The sovereignty they discuss is dependent on a different kind of representation, the representation of essentialized desires/wants; this notion of representation is open to the same general critique as political representation but this point is not a relevant one to pursue here. (For an important modern discussion of representation in political theory see Pitkin 1967.)

The criticisms that can be made of the notion of a sovereignty or rights is *ipso facto* a defence of industrial democracy in the sense of being a defence of *some* degree of autonomy for producers in production decisions. The criticism of a 'sovereignty of capacity' is also a defence of industrial democracy in the sense that some degree of producer autonomy is inescapable because of the insuperable obstacle to any centralized planning mechanisms presented by the quantity of information necessary to plan each and every decision.

The latter argument is hardly new but it remains important. Actual planning systems have 'recognized' this limitation by always being based on some degree of iteration between planner and planned and by the granting of a degree of autonomy to decentralized entities – locales, sectors, or whatever. The crucial problem of enforcement cannot however be readily overcome – how is a formal agreement by the enterprise to the plan to be policed? In many ways planning systems produce the same problems of regulating the activity of *private* enterprise in capitalist countries, which are discussed in Chapter 7 (though of course without the regulatory capacities of either agencies of socialist education or the KGB).

The argument here is not that socialists, because of the weakness of the sovereignty claims, should favour 'total' autonomy of production units. Indeed the very idea of 'total autonomy' is surely an impossible one – no enterprise can be wholly independent of conditions outside itself relating to markets, finance, etc. The argument is on the one hand simply that the question of the relation of individual units of production and the planning mechanisms cannot be posed at the level of sovereignty. On the other hand a strength of the Webbs/Cole argument is that the terrain of the argument is that which is appropriate, the terrain of politics, where the question of enterprise autonomy is not one which can be solved by searching for appropriate forms of administration adequate to the 'rational' organization of the economy. As Littlejohn (1979) rightly argues, too often the vexed question of appropriate planning mechanisms under socialist relations of production is posed as a 'technical' question, a problem soluble in isolation from any argument about the political forces engaged in and political consequences of struggles over appropriate planning systems.

On that terrain of politics what are the appropriate terms of the argument? So far Cole's position has been put forward as a negative one – a refutation of the Webbs' claim. More positively Cole proposes a *right* of producers to control as a consequence of their function as producers. This appears an attractive proposition from a socialist position – a legal right to a say in the control of the enterprise. Such a right would, like any right, not be an absolute, unproblematic entity, it would have to be subject to certain qualifying conditions, for example length of employment. The advantage of such a right would lie in providing a separate arena of struggle, that is a legal one, where the functioning of enterprises would be open to debate and challenge. Thus such a right would provide one of the multiple sites for scrutiny of the enterprise which would on the one hand evade the claims of sovereignty (not based on rights as citizens) but would provide *one* means whereby the 'general interest' (in the form of laws) can intervene in the operations of individual enterprises. The problem of such a right is, as Hirst argues (1980), its derivation from ontological doctrines where such rights are conceived as the *recognition* of something already in existence, prior and privileged attributes of human subjects. As against this the only rights which can be considered helpful in the context of industrial democracy are ones which are specifically constructed by law, pertain to persons only of a certain status and are limited and conditional.

II

The second objection of the Webbs, that based on the alleged characteristics of modern industry raises a series of problems which are generally much less focused than those relating to sovereignty. Here Cole provides only a partial contestation of the Webbs' arguments.

The Webbs' position has a strong if partial parallel with that of Marx (see Chapter 1) in the idea that the supersession of craft industry by machine industry brings about a fundamental change in the character of industrial production, resulting in a subordination of labour to capital which undercuts the possibility of industrial democracy. This comes about in modern industry by the simultaneous reduction of the skills and the autonomy in work of the 'average worker'.

The parallel here is a parallel of two historicisms with different paths to a similar outcome. The Webbs' 'technicist' version sees the growth of machine industry as a result of technological change which in turn dictates the character of the division of labour. The Marxist version sees the technological changes as subordinate to the contradictory social relations of capitalism, so that the division of labour is an effect of capital accumulation in the context of worker antagonism to exploitative social relations which can, at least partially, be weakened by 'de-skilling'.[4]

The Marxist version is more precisely specified than that of the Webbs. Marx, as argued in Chapter 1, at least breaks the process down into component aspects with on the one hand production as the production of commodities and on the other production as an integration of diverse but co-operative labours. In addition the Marxist version makes appeal to the 'social' as opposed to the 'technical' basis of the division of labour. But this 'social' is in effect a kind of meta-rationality which imposes itself on capitalist production, interrupted only by the indeterminate effects of 'class struggle' (of which argument the classic example is of course Braverman 1974).

A recent powerful version of the non-Marxist aspect of this argument is Fox (1974). He argues that (p. 211)

> In work relations, a reduction of discretion is accompanied by increasing supervision, inspection, checking, monitoring or other forms of policing the prescribed elements. This was explained in

terms of the decline in personal involvement by the self as discretionary obligations gave way to prescribed obligations for which only obedience is required.

Now whatever the force of this argument, it does rely on a premise concerning the evolution of job contents which (as Fox recognized, p. 191) is not well supported by the range of historical evidence that would be required to make the thesis a convincing one.[5] This is not to dispute that such a policy of de-skilling and reducing worker autonomy has been embedded in a number of theorists of the enterprise, most famously of course Taylor, but there is no good reason to move from those programmatic statements of individual managerial ideologies to the practices of the generality of enterprises (see e.g. Nelson 1974). Cole himself (1955), using just skill as the criterion, provided evidence that there is no clear evidence of a major shift in nineteenth- and early twentieth-century Britain towards the kind of low autonomy, unskilled jobs which, if this thesis is to be supported, would have to be becoming the norm in industrial societies. He argues (p. 37–8) that only the very first phase of the industrial revolution saw the homogenization and general de-skilling of the labour force, later phases having been characterized by increasing differentiation of types of labour for a substantial proportion of the workforce. (This led into a critique of Marxism for its neglect of the role of 'brainworkers' – see for example Cole (1920b, p. 67).)

For Marxism this thesis of the growth of an increasingly homogenized and 'dehumanized' workforce is paralleled by a positive aspect which sees these conditions as politically favourable because functional to the creation of a mass political consciousness amenable to socialism. Three points can be made on this thesis. One is that in a modified form it can be accepted – if it is argued firstly that large-scale factory organization is favourable (though certainly not a *sine qua non*) to mass trade unionism, and secondly that trade unionism, under certain historical conditions, has been a major means whereby socialist ideology has been propagated. Such a qualified thesis does of course break the close connection commonly alleged between factory industry and socialist politics.

Secondly, and this is a point raised elsewhere in the book, this Marxist historicism works as if the organization of *industrial* production were clearly the crucial aspect of the organization of production in general. But this certainty cannot be established quantitatively as industrial workers, however broadly defined, are a very much a minority of all workers in Britain and all other advanced capitalist countries. Even if we accept the common though contested Marxist privileging of industrial workers as 'productive' it is not at all clear why this privileging on the basis of a theory of value should lead to a *political* privileging. To put this point slightly differently: even if the most extreme version of the de-skilling thesis were accepted, either this would have to be argued to relate to the whole of the working population (shop and office workers, teachers, social workers, etc.) or its relevance to a large mass of the population would be small.

Thirdly, most of the discussion of industrial democracy (including that of the Webbs and Cole) privileges manufacturing industry in a way which seems theoretically insupportable and politically perverse. Industrial democracy, if it is to embrace the mass of the workforce, must presumably be industrial democracy in the office, the local hairdresser, the corner shop, the school as well as the factory.

Cole in many ways shares the view of the Webbs in treating the organization of production and the division of labour as dictated by rational economic calculation. As a consequence they both produce an unequivocal role for the expert (Wright 1979, e.g. p. 66), this role being an effect of a rational division of labour which 'gives' various kinds of expertise to exclusive sets of agents. Any challenge to this need not of course be based on a utopian conception that without capitalist mystification production would be an open book, accessible without preparation to all. A firmer base for such a challenge is necessary and would seem to be twofold.

First that whilst technique in the sense of machines/production processes does put constraints on the forms of organization of labour, these constraints are not so narrow as to provide no possibility of alternative modes of organization aimed to combine efficient production with an 'appropriate' division of labour (and this is of course to leave aside the extremely complex question of how far industrial technique itself must be a function of a taken-for-granted division of labour rather than purely 'technological/scientific' criteria). Secondly that the 'appropriate' division of labour will be constrained by the distribution of competences amongst agents in the production process, but this distribution need not be treated as in any way sacrosanct, but something which itself is always the object of transformation by socialists. Arguments about 'expertise' must then avoid the question of expertise with the existence of immutable categories of workers.

A second major aspect of the conception of 'modern industry' which underlies the Webbs' position is that relating to scale. Here again the Webbs' position is now a common one: the scale of modern industrial production is read both as a necessity (in line with the division of labour) and as an obstacle to democracy.

In contrast Cole provides at least the beginnings of an alternative position. Firstly Cole, whilst going along with the common argument that the scale of modern industrial production is *technologically* determined, points out that certain kinds of new technology may favour smaller-scale production. 'Large-scale industry . . . might, as electric power, easily divisible and cheaply transmitted, continues to develop, disappear even as machinery increased' (1919, p. 232). He also hints that even with existing technology 'the tendency in the past has even been to let the scale of production outrun the limits of efficiency'.

Secondly Cole suggests a distinction between the efficient scale for trading and that efficient directly in industrial production – that is, he argues that the scale appropriate to different aspects of production processes may vary. This is an important lead into the third point – that scale is important for democracy.

> Make a man a voter among voters in a democratic community; it is at least a half-truth that the measure of control he will have will vary inversely to the total number of votes. So, in the workshop, the control of the individual will be real in most cases only if the workshop is small, unless, as in a coal mine, only the simplest and most uniform questions have, as a rule, to be decided. Wherever at all a complex government is needed, the National Guild will need to be broken up into the smallest possible units (1919, p. 233).

All three of these points could be reinforced and extended (see also Tomlinson 1980a). Within the confines of Cole's own arguments other kinds of recent technology which would seem to be compatible with small-scale production can be pointed to, for example plastic moulding, micro-chip technology. More radical is the argument that Cole's 'technological determinism' is misplaced and that a great deal of the scale of modern industry is linked not to some (capitalist)

58

economic rationality but to (above all) the *financial* organization of capitalist economies. This argument could be found in both 'orthodox' economic literature (especially Prais 1976) and in a slightly different form in post-Marxist accounts (Cutler *et al.* 1977, 1978). The argument, broadly speaking, is that any capitalist economy based on general credit availability (with few restrictions as to type of asset financed or period of credit) will favour the larger over the smaller firm. This will arise both because of 'economies of scale' in financing (lower costs per unit of finance for larger firms) and because financial institutions use size as an index of risk in assessing potential creditors. This will add to the differential effect of varying profit levels on firms' expansion, given that so much investment (especially in Britain) is financed from ploughed back profits. In addition particular institutional arrangements, for example a large role for institutional investors in share purchases, may accentuate these effects. This is the case where pension funds have such large inflows of funds that these can be disbursed with the management resources of the fund only in very large units, and hence to large firms.

The implication of these arguments is that Cole's rather vague feeling that the scale of capitalist production may not be necessary for efficient production can be sharpened. *Much* of the expansion of the scale of the capitalist enterprise (i.e. the legal entity) is to do with the financial system and not any 'technical' rationality. Empirical support for this is given by Prais's data showing that most of the growth of large firms in Britain in the twentieth century has been due to the growth of multi-plant enterprises rather than growth in the scale of plants. On the assumption that *most* economies of scale exist at plant level (see Pratten 1971), their role in enterprise expansion would seem to be greatly exaggerated. This is not to doubt that there are some planning, managerial and marketing economies which are realized by unified possession of multi-plant entities, but the evidence for their existence on a large scale, a scale sufficient to 'explain' the scale of modern enterprises, does not seem to exist.

Cole's second point raises a central issue for any socialist account of the capitalist enterprise – the need to 'deconstruct' this entity. This point is taken up in much greater detail in Chapter 7. Here let it suffice to note that Cole's point suggests the necessity of conceiving the enterprise not as a unity, its different aspects determined by some central principle, but a conglomeration of different practices, linked to each other but in a variety of ways which may be complementary or contradictory. In relation to size for example this means that 'size' of the enterprise has no one meaning but depends on the particular function and argument involved. For purposes of maximizing democracy for example the size which may be appropriate may be 'organizational size' (that is a level where certain decisions are made) or legal size (the size of the legally constituted company). In some cases these sizes may be the same (the small firm) and in others widely divergent. The size which is pertinent can only be decided in relation to the object involved; for example in relation to democracy 'size' in the sense of units of organization may be crucial, as in Cole's argument.

Thirdly Cole links the scale of industry to democracy. He does not provide a rationale for such a position, but one can readily be given. The danger is of basing this on some kind of moral essentialism where humans are seen as essentially 'more at home' in small-scale environments (Schumacher 1973). A much more interesting liberal position is in Goodman (1969). A surer foundation would seem to be to base arguments for a link between small size and effective democracy on competence. Thus it can be argued that if it is to be effective (as measured by participation by a large proportion of the constituency) democracy must require a minimum possible level of competence on the part of all agents in the democratic process. This competence is likely to be partly a function of the quantity of information acquired by agents. The assimilation of adequate information and skills will therefore put a finite limit on the domain of effective democracy. Of course this raises a host of problems (see Chapter 7) but the point here is largely to stress that Cole's breaking up of the common socialist position that scale equals efficiency and that democracy must adapt to this overweening necessity is a vital positive part of his arguments and one that should be built upon.

One could in this context extend Cole's point that most arguments against industrial democracy could also be used against political democracy. Political democracy involves both electing certain persons and then subsequently obeying them, without obviously creating intolerable psychological strain on those doing the obeying.

The final point of the Webbs' assertions against industrial democracy is both the weakest and also the most difficult to refute. Whereas the previous points were founded on either political theory or a clear-cut historicism, this third element remains at the level of a psychological 'law'. It is far from clear what could count as a refutation of such a universal imperative. The best that can be done is to make two empirical points.

First much of the hostility of the Webbs to associations of producers was based on the research done for Beatrice Potter's book (1891/1933, Ch. V). This surveyed the lack of success of the large number of producer co-operatives established in England from the time of Owen onwards. This catalogue of failure is concluded by arguments that three major reasons accounted for this failure. First, a lack of capital condemned many co-operatives (see on this Chapter 2 above). Secondly a 'want of custom' which Potter put down to the focus of the co-operatives on production and their ignorance and unconcern with sales. Thirdly, and most important here, an 'absence of administrative discipline' was said to be the most significant factor leading to co-operatives' demise (p. 152). Now two points can be simply made in relation to these arguments. On the one hand the first two points would seem to provide good reasons for the failure of many of the co-operatives Potter discusses, as indeed they do for the failure of more modern examples (which of course is not assent that such problems are *inevitable* with producer co-operatives). Secondly even where there were clear management failings in co-operatives Potter does not demonstrate that this resulted from the infringement of her psychological law. Management succeeds and fails in all types of production enterprise, so there seems little good reason for asserting that failure is linked to co-operation itself, though clearly this does provide its own peculiar problems for management.

The second general point that can be made is that where systems of elective relations between workers and managers have been instituted (notably in Yugoslavia) this does *not* seem to have led to the 'psychological impossibility' suggested by the Webbs (see for example Tannenbaum *et al.* 1974). Whilst the Yugoslav economy faces serious problems, these do not seem to include a major breakdown of work discipline – indeed this seems much more to be the case in other East European economies (especially the Soviet Union and Poland) where of course such elective relations do not exist.

This chapter has clearly not dealt with the institutional details of any system of industrial democracy. Whilst this is much needed, it would seem to require as a precondition an examination of many of the assumptions upon which discussion of such democracy is commonly based. This chapter has tried to make a contribution to such an examination. The objective has not been to suggest that Cole 'solved' all the theoretical problems of industrial democracy, far from it. But in certain key respects, especially that stemming from his discussion of representation and sovereignty, he provided a vastly superior starting point for socialist discussion of industrial democracy than the Webbs.

NOTES

1 Unfortunately there is no published direct confrontation between these factions. The issues were no doubt discussed by the Fabian Research Committee on the Control of Industry but the critique of guild socialism promised by the Webbs in one of the reports of this Committee did not appear in that format. See Webbs (1914) and M. Cole (1952, p. 13).
2 This line of argument is similar to that of Marx's account of the genesis of the 'despotism of the factory'. See Chapter 1 above.
3 Here, as elsewhere, I use 'men' to fit in with the quotations which follow but conscious of the sexism implied.
4 The concept of skill is of course a highly ambiguous one. For one attempt to specify it in a serious way and use this specification to analyse the skill requirements of forms of factory production see Bright (1958).
5 Fox's one source (Friedmann 1964) itself offers only a very narrow range of evidence for the 'de-skilling' thesis.

CHAPTER FOUR

Nationalization: socialist panacea?

Since at least the First World War nationalization and public ownership have been the touchstone of socialist positions in Britain (but not of course elsewhere in Europe, e.g. Scandinavia, on which see Castles 1978). With all the necessary nuances and qualifications that must be accepted on such a broad generalization, socialists them-selves have largely supported the existence of such a clear dividing line. With all the multifarious groupings, ideologies and politics grouped under its banner, perhaps *only* the commitment to national-ization has served to unite British socialism – albeit often only at the level of doctrine. For example it is far from clear that Gaitskell's well-known 'revisionist' speech to the 1959 Labour Party Conference (1959, pp. 110–13) implied any substantive change in Labour Party *policy*, but by questioning the centrality of nationalization to socialist politics he struck at the heart of what many Labour Party members saw as the *raison d'être* of the party (see ibid., pp. 114–55). Clause IV of the Labour Party's constitution, with its commitment to the 'common ownership of the means of production, distribution and exchange' remains the only part of that constitution printed on Labour Party membership cards. Beyond the Labour Party the central, continuous and bitter criticism of Labour policy has been of its failure to live up to this commitment, not the nature of the commitment itself (e.g. Miliband 1973, pp. 350ff.).

The socialist consensus that whatever else socialism might be about, it is irredeemably about nationalization and public ownership does not imply any consensus about either the nature or objectives of this policy. As Pollard (1979, pp. 184–5) has written of the long history of proposals to nationalize the banks in Britain:

> it emerged and disappeared from time to time as a component of different policy packages, without being firmly based on a tradition of its own. . . . More significant still is the discontinuity which can be observed in the justification, rather than the proposals themselves. . . . Beginning with redistributive justice and economic power, we move to efficiency, the maintenance of employment, the prevention of poverty, the control over foreign policy, the planning of industry, efficiency and low cost in banking, the prevention of fraud, the reduction in nepotism, the development of long-term investment, and many others besides from time to time.

A similar heterogeneity of meanings could be applied to most of the other nationalization proposals which have engaged socialist arguments (see e.g. Barry 1965). No doubt this can be read as evidence of typical British pragmatism, making concessions to rhetoric whilst getting on with the 'real business'. But this is not adequate. Nationalization may not determine every policy proposal that socialists make, but it does have powerful effects on the way socialist argument is conducted, and certainly it cannot easily be separated from other socialist positions. Most important of all it provides a crucial part of how the *goal* of socialism is defined, and therefore, at the same time, a crucial part of what is seen as defining *socialist* politics as clearly distinct from all others.

The first part of this chapter is concerned not with how this domination of British socialism by nationalization/public ownership came about (on this see the brief comments in the introduction above and Barry, especially Ch. 5) but about its status as doctrine – what arguments does it depend upon and support, and what in turn are the strengths and weaknesses of these arguments? Clearly this involves very general questions about the status of socialism because nationalization has in Britain 'the appearance of a programme inspired by abstract socialist ideas' rather than merely a response to current exigencies and examples (Katzarov 1964, p. 79).

Central to the argument for nationalization has been a particular conception of property. Nationalization as a policy assumes that the legal status of property is a crucial determinant of the organization and use of that property. Thus the distinction between public and private property is seen as in principle a clear-cut, unambiguous one and a distinction with clear-cut and unambiguous consequences. G.D.H. Cole (1932, Ch. XII) recognizes the problem but makes a sharp distinction between private companies with 'public powers' and other joint stock companies which seems unsustainable – see further below, pp. 66–8.

The public/private property argument has clear links with other dichotomies within political philosophy, such as 'state and civil society', where each of these is conceived of as having its own separate domain and characteristic practices. In the case of property in the means of production such black and white distinctions seem difficult to sustain. 'Private' property can never give a wholly unconstrained capacity on the part of the owner or owners to dispose of such means. Setting means of production to work always involves combining these means with other elements – above all labour – which necessarily puts some bounds on what way those means of production are going to be used. The very separation of means of production from those who work with them (paradoxically perhaps) constructs limits on the way those means can be used, because that use is itself conditional on a 're-combination' in some form of worker and means of production.[1] This is a very general point but it is important to stress that it does not depend on any specific forms of organization, etc. amongst either capital or labour.

More concretely the characteristic modern form of private property in the means of production – the joint stock company – is by definition regulated to some degree by the legal instance, because the joint stock company is itself created as a (legal) subject by the state. The very fact of the joint stock company being a separate legal entity (and an exceptional one: it is explicitly set up as outside mainstream common law – its liability is limited for example – so of necessity there is an apparatus of legislation) *necessarily* severs any simple relation between the company's shareholders and control of the assets which belong to the company *qua* company. The status granted to joint stock companies always involves certain conditions being fulfilled in return, that is conditions are attached to the disposition of the means of production which the corporate joint stock enterprise owns. Of course the stringency of these conditions can vary enormously, and in some cases amounts to little effective constraint. But the general point is that to base arguments about nationalization and the disposition of property on a distinction between public and private property as if there were a clear-cut distinction is in principle misleading.

The doctrinal strength of this distinction has depended partly on a conception that private property has characteristic forms of policy and organization, and thus legal ownership *is* significant because of its consequences. One aspect of this has been discussed in Chapter 2, in relation to the common Marxist argument that profit-maximizing by capitalist firms inscribes necessary forms and tendencies on the operation of those firms. I have argued there that such an argument cannot be sustained in the absence of specification of the mechanisms whereby calculation of profit acts as a determining principle in relation to every area of decision-making in the firm.

The same point can be generalized in relation to the notion of private property versus public. This legal distinction of itself would seem to have no necessary consequences for the model of operation, organization, etc. of the firm – both public and private firms can be 'profit maximizing'. This is not to argue that an alteration of legal status of property is wholly irrelevant to its manner of use and disposition, but that this cannot be specified separate from (a) the particular objective in pursuit of which the legal status of that property is to be changed and (b) the particular mechanisms whereby legal changes have effects on the locus and character of decision-making within the firm and consequently on the practices employed.

Such a way of posing the problem would cut across some of the ways nationalization has been argued about in Britain. For example the dispute between Gaitskell and his allies and the adherents of an undiluted Clause IV centres on the question of whether nationalization was a 'means' or an 'end'. For Gaitskell nationalization was desirable only in so far as it helped to achieve 'social justice', 'the classless society', etc.; for his opponents it was an end in itself, because it defined socialism. Both of these positions, in very different ways, assumed that there was a general relation (albeit vague) between nationalization and the attainment of socialist objectives, without any attempt at specifying how changes in legal status might affect other practices. In his Fabian pamphlet, Gaitskell (1956) was wholly unclear whether the shortcomings of nationalized industries have much to do with that legal status.

The very legalistic notions of property inscribed in much of the debate about nationalization have as their counterpart very legalistic (constitutionalist) notions of politics. In the present context this led to a conception of the state as the appropriate body for owning industry because only this body could truly represent the general public as opposed to private interests. Thus nationalization was pursued as a policy despite a strong hostility to the state as an employer, not because the state was conceived of as the central political power but because it was deemed to represent the community (Katzarov 1964, p. 151). From a *legal* viewpoint this clearly makes sense – constitutionally the state does work for the 'general interest'. The political sense of this position is much less clear.

British socialism in particular has always been imbued (or at least its rhetoric has) with a strong undertow of anti-statism. The squaring of this with state ownership under nationalization took the form of the public corporation. A clear legal distinction was made between the state and nationalized undertakings, and the strength of the distinction was reinforced by placing these nationalized undertakings under the system of civil law, especially contract, and not administrative law (Katzarov 1964). In this way nationalized corporations can be seen as much less innovative than the joint stock company.

The effect of this was a strange hybrid which combined a clear legal status as state property, a constitutional subordination to parliament, with an effectively unaccountable organizational structure. This hybrid is discussed in detail in the second half of this chapter, but the point here is that the space for its existence as the preferred form of nationalized industry was in *part* the consequence of the theoretical arguments upon which nationalization *in general* rested. These arguments may accurately be characterized as *essentialist*, in the sense of implying that the practices both of private/public property and of the state can be deduced from their legal/constitutional essences.

Such arguments were profoundly conservative in that they did not seek to problematize existing constitutional and political theories, but attempted to weave socialist argument into these theories. The arguments for nationalization were also profoundly conservative in a different sense, in that they commonly rested upon a strong continuity between the nationalized industries and their predecessor joint stock companies.

In part this similarity depended upon a characteristic evolutionism which may be most strongly articulated in Marx but which imbued much of the Left from Fabians leftwards. This evolutionism saw the growth of joint stock companies in general and monopolies in particular as steps on the road to socialism. 'Economic power' (conceived of largely in legal terms) was thus highly concentrated, but in private hands (e.g. TUC 1944, pp. 397–8). Nationalization would mean the displacement of this private power into public hands but beyond that it might not much affect the organization of the company.

Many commentators in Britain noted this clear parallel between the joint stock company and the public corporation. Most commonly this was done by Liberals concerned to stress the non-importance of the traditional socialist distinction between public and private property (see e.g. Liberal Party 1928, pp. 76–7, replied to by Cole 1932, Ch. XII; Keynes 1933, pp. 314–16). But this was not just a polemical point because by and large socialists did *not* challenge this parallel precisely because of the legalistic basis of their doctrine which suggested that most of what was wrong with the joint stock company was the epiphenomena of its legal essence. Displace that, it was argued, and the major step had been taken.

Thus it is characteristic of socialist argument, particularly between the wars (see Barry 1965, Chs 10–13), that the questions of nationalization and rationalization (re-organization) were not closely linked. For example the existing division of labour within the corporate sector was largely taken for granted, except by G.D.H. Cole (1929). This is important because once the question of what constitutes a particular industry to be nationalized is raised as a problem the relation between the nationalized concern and preceding corporate forms becomes problematic. Moreover, once this is rendered problematic the conception of the private corporation as having an unambiguous domain which can be transferred into public hands is also undercut. These consequences can be seen in Cole's arguments (1929, pp. 137–42). Once he asks the question 'what is the coal industry?' he is led into arguing that what is at stake in the argument is policy in a particular area, e.g. coal-getting. Once posed in this way the clear link between nationalization of '*the*' existing coal industry and this particular activity is broken, the point of simply tranferring the existing organization into public entities becomes unclear, that is it is not clear that the same policy objectives could not be achieved with the industry remaining in private ownership.

A final problem which arises here is the notion of 'economic power' which is part of the socialist argument. Power in the enterprise is seen in terms of its possession by particular agents, in the case of the joint stock company largely as being in the hands of the board of directors.

Once again this is a legalistic definition, but it might also be polemically characterized as a *totalitarian* one. By this is meant that the image of the firm conjured up by many socialist discussions of the capitalist enterprise is one where there is a clear-cut locus of control which at least in principle has the capacity to make sure its decisions are carried out throughout the firm. This again would appear to be an inhibition to the understanding of the firm. Much better it would seem to conceive the firm (as any organization) as a set of decision-making arenas, articulated with another in a variety of ways but with no wholly clear-cut hierarchy of super- and subordination. In this way the question of 'power' in the firm doesn't arise in the same way. Rather the question always hinges on what arenas will be involved (and what will be the consequences for other arenas) in obtaining any particular objective. Nationalization can then be addressed as a means of changing the terms of struggle in one or more arenas within the firm rather than a general relocation of 'power'. Clearly there is a complicity between the notion of power-as-sovereignty and the multi-purpose way that nationalization has been argued for as in the quote from Pollard at the beginning of this chapter. Achieving 'power' is seen as the pathway to all ends – as bestowing omnipotence. Given this it is not surprising that nationalization is *always* a disappointment to socialists – it simply cannot achieve the multiplicity of goals set for it.

This last point may be taken to exemplify the general argument here. Nationalization is always a policy which is 'overdetermined', the consequence of many different and divergent arguments and not the simple deduction from a single premise. Nevertheless the major positions it depends upon and entails have been argued above to be on the whole inadequate both in terms of their characterization of the capitalist firm and the appropriate politics to transform it. Conceptions of global status like 'the state', 'the public interest', 'power' would seem to lie behind much of that inadequacy, a point which is taken up again in the conclusion.

Nationalization itself implies nothing about the form of organization of the industry concerned, and in consequence agreement on the demand for nationalization could (and does) conceal radically divergent conceptions of what such forms should be. Thus for example both Cole and the Webbs in the arguments discussed in Chapter 3 assumed that nationalization would be the legal 'shell' of the widely different forms they favoured.

In the debates over the form that nationalization should take, the proponents of the 'new form', the public corporation, constructed from the late 1920s onwards a clear, double-stranded tradition which they saw their new form as displacing. Emphases differed but generally this tradition was seen as consisting of 'State department nationalisation with the Minister responsible for management' (Morrison 1933, p. 193) (or similar municipalization for local industries and services) or 'workers control' (LP Conference 1932, p. 213) which meant, to varying degrees, direct labour representation on the controlling agencies of the nationalized industries. Such a characterization of earlier socialist positions no doubt greatly exaggerates their homogeneity (see Barry 1965, Pt I), but the concern here is not the accuracy or otherwise of this characterization but the way in which arguments *against* these positions provided the basis for British socialism's most important debate about the form nationalization should take. This debate took place between 1929 and 1945, but mainly in the first few years of the 1930s. Prior to World War I most discussion of nationalization had been about the terms of compensation offered to previous owners of nationalized industries and only with the rise of syndicalism, guild socialism and industrial unionism was there much concern with questions of management and control of industry (G.D.H. Cole 1931, p. 395). However (as seen in Chapter 3) most of this debate took nationalization for granted and raised issues about the possibility of industrial democracy *in general* rather than relating this specifically to problems of nationalization. In relation to the form of nationalization such debates did not arise much until the first Labour government came to formulate its programme, above all for London Transport, in the wake of the election victory of 1929.

Before looking at these debates a couple of general points should be stressed about how such debates should be viewed. On the one hand it would be grossly rationalistic to see the victory of the notion of the public corporation as *the* form of nationalization simply as the consequence of theoretical debate in complete isolation from the exigencies of the period concerned. Equally, it is important not to reduce the whole movement of the debate to a 'pragmatism', where the unworldly socialist doctrine is modified in the face of worldly facts. Current exigencies did play a large part in the triumph of the public corporation idea, but these exigencies were always seen in relation to a pre-existing discourse of 'socialism' – that is the 'brute facts' themselves were constructed by and for socialist doctrine. Here we attempt to avoid both these traps. As the interest here is in socialist doctrine, the focus will be on how such doctrine was transformed, how current concerns were inserted into it, and how general positions on appropriate socialist policies developed from this complex set of interactions.

Whilst the Labour Party may be said to have been 'converted' to the public corporation by the end of the 1930s, this conversion was the 'product of neither conference decision nor of long natured plan, fully discussed in the organisations of the Labour Movement' (Hanson 1954, p. 203). Discussion of the public corporation was not well focused and with clear points of reference, but consisted of many *ad hoc* arguments, partial debates and widespread fudging of differences. Nevertheless within this a number of clear lines of argument emerge as crucial. In enumerating and discussing these we will concentrate on those which seem most significant to the development of socialist argument.

The first of these is the notion of interests. Morrison, in attacking those who opposed his notion of ministers appointing boards of public corporations on the 'grounds of ability', and who wanted instead direct Labour representation, argued that to concede this would make it impossible to resist the claims of other interests to be similarly represented (LP Conference 1932, p. 213; Morrison 1933, pp. 182–3). At one level such a position was perfectly comprehensible – the 1929 Labour government was a minority government dependent on Liberal support, which might well have made a 'bias' towards Labour representation politically difficult to sustain. It was perfectly understandable that many socialists (e.g. LP Conference 1932, p. 216) would resist this notion of workers in an industry as just one amongst several interests, and in attempting to develop this resistance they raised more general problems about how the notion of interests can function in discussions of the enterprise.

C. Dukes, who attacked the Morrisonian notions of the public corporation, argued that:

You have got to have machinery, and that machinery in the initial stages, I do not care how you select your men, will represent interests. They will go into the management of the industry with certain preconceived ideas. I would rather face that fairly then make a pretence that a man who has spent his life in the industry can completely shed all those interests that have made him what he is when he enters a board of control, merely because we happen to change its name. (LP Conference 1932, p. 206)

Clearly this is a highly subjective notion of interest which is similar in meaning to the everyday notion of 'bias'. Such a subjective notion of interest is also apparent in Morrison (e.g. 1933, p. 157). Posing the problem in this way would seem necessarily to lead into a quagmire, into an endless debate over whether such-and-such a person has such-and-such interests. This would appear never to be resolvable because it is very unclear what could count as evidence of such subjective intent.

Focusing on such arguments, the opponents of the Morrisonian public corporation did not strongly contest the much more important argument of proponents, that the public corporations form was constructed so as to work for the general public interest (sometimes called the interests of socialism (LP Conference 1932, p. 208)) as against sectional interests (Morrison 1933, p. 157). The weakness of this kind of justification for non-representation of particular interests is that it assumes that the fact of 'non-representation' will itself guarantee pursuit of the (unproblematic) general interest. The question of how this pursuit is going to be monitored and controlled is evaded by the invocation of the doctrine of parliamentary sovereignty, so that by giving the minister the right delegated by parliament to appoint board members the public will in fact be adequately represented. The question of parliamentary sovereignty will be taken up directly, but clearly a defence of interest-based board members *can* be mounted on the grounds that only by some mode of representation can machinery be established which creates some effective accountability of those members. The question of account-ability of board members is raised on occasion in the 1930s debate (e.g. LP Conference 1932, p. 215), but this is linked solely to particular issues (in this case the role of the BBC in the 1931 general election) rather than the general questions of organization. This clearly does not say anything about the question of which interests are to be represented and in what proportions. This question, though obviously important, in part depends on the prior establishment of the legitimacy (in socialist terms) of interest representation as a basis for nationalization. As has been stressed, one way of establishing this legitimacy is to bring to the forefront the actual mechanisms of accountability generated by interest representation, in opposition to the wholly abstract notion that the public interest can be somehow guaranteed largely by the absence of organized interests.

This abstract notion depends in part on the doctrine of parliamentary sovereignty. As the TUC typically argued (1944, p. 400), 'In relation to corporations of this type, it is essential that responsibility to the public shall be maintained by the appointment of the members of the governing body by a Minister responsible to Parliament' and (p. 411) 'Ultimate control over the policy and direction of a public industry must be exercised by Parliament as representative of the community in general.'

Dahl (1947, p. 877) argues that the defence of parliament as sovereign representative of the people's will was the most important Fabian argument against workers' control. The conception of parliamentary sovereignty in the sense of its representative status giving that body rights was criticized by G.D.H. Cole around the end of the First World War as already discussed in Chapter 3. His discussion of nationalization reasserts some of this critique, the 'nominal' responsibility of the public corporations to parliament must be accompanied by an effective responsibility to a functional body co-ordinating the activities of these corporations. A central body is needed for the control of *economic* policy: 'Until that is provided, no really satisfactory form can be developed for the socialisation of any enterprise' (Cole 1929, p. 136). Hinted at here is the argument of *Self Government in Industry* (1919), that true representation can only be on the specific functions, not a general representation of men's wills. But this is coupled with a conception of society as where representatives of the people make laws and these laws are 'the ultimate determinant of social policy' (ibid., p. 169). This opens up the second strand of the critique of parliamentary sovereignty (and the crucial one here), a critique based on parliament's *capacities*. The central argument derived from Hindess (1980) discussed in Chapter 3 is that parliamentary sovereignty can never be realized because no one body can exhaustively determine the activities of allegedly subordinate bodies. Law-making capacity in no way guarantees the legislative assembly effective control of the multifarious agencies over which it has the constitutional right to assert its powers.

This general point is applicable to nationalized industries. Parliament may have greater or lesser control over the activities of nationalized industries but this control must always leave some degree of autonomy to those industries. No imaginable parliament would have the enormous capacity necessary to determine every decision of a nationalized industry. If such autonomy is inescapable then to argue that only parliament has the right to control the activities of a nationalized corporation means in effect defending an irresponsible status for that corporation. Here again one can assert the legitimate role of interests in acting as agencies of accountability for such corporations and filling part of the role that is *impossible* for parliament to perform.

The incapacity of parliament effectively to subordinate all the actions of public corporations was recognized by proponents of such corporations. A central part of their case, against both the 'workers' control' and 'department of state' arguments, was that management is a job for experts, for trained personnel free from both the claims of inexpert interest and interference by a non-expert parliament (Morrison 1933, pp. 137–8; TUC 1944, p. 400). In this way there was a straightforward movement in the argument from assertion of the necessity of expertise to the claim that only the public corporation form could give proper weight to such expertise.

On the one side this meant an attack on the capacities of civil servants to wield such expertise. Morrison (e.g. 1933, p. 136) argued that the Post Office, as the classic case of direct ministerial responsibility and civil service administration, was successful only because its operations were of a 'fairly regular and systematic character'. Transport, by contrast, required an adaptability and flexibility which could only be provided by expert managers. Equally this need for flexibility was seen as an argument against Labour representatives, who would, because of their lack of knowledge, make the enterprise less efficient than would be the case if left to managers (ibid., pp. 182–3).

Socialists at the time strongly combated such arguments. Firstly of course there was the legitimate, albeit wholly polemical, point that the use of arguments about expertise against democracy *in politics* was in principle no different from its use in talking about nationalized corporations, and no more defensible (TUC 1931, p. 437) (this was a point often made by Cole in his guild socialist writings). More substantial was the argument that the issue was not one of the necessity of expertise – that could be readily accepted by everyone – but that this necessity did not mean that those possessing the expertise should control policy. 'There was a place for the administrator and there was a place for the technical expert, but it was not at the top but below, acting under the instructions of the workers who should have the control and direct the policy' (TUC 1933, p. 375). At one level, and leaving aside here questions about the distribution of expertise amongst particular agents, this was an adequate reply to those who proposed the rule of the expert. But it did rely on the assumption of an unambiguous separation between policy issues, decided by workers' representatives, and policy implementation, pursued by experts. It seems difficult to sustain such a distinction because 'policy' would seem always in part precisely to depend on how the means of implementation are deployed – there is no hard and fast dividing line. However, this is not to say that structures based on attempts to separate these elements are not feasible, as long as it is accepted that the bodies which control these separate functions will never be simply superordinate and subordinate, but always also in a position of contesting each other's powers.

Such a separation of function is of course embodied in the German joint stock company form, the *Aktiengesellschaft*, with its supervisory board for policy and a subordinate managerial board, with from 1919 the former having labour representatives on it (a pattern of course re-established in West Germany after the Third Reich). This form of company structure was suggested by G.D.H. Cole (1931, pp. 403–5) with a part-time council of control composed mainly of 'representatives of groups concerned', a substantial part being workers, and below this a board of full-time managerial staff. Morrison responded to such suggestions by saying that such an organization would be 'a heaven and hell of management' and that no one would want to serve on the lower board. This of course completely ignored the German experience, which, whatever its problems, does not seem to have suffered from an unwillingness of managers to work within such a framework.

Perhaps here in particular one should be aware of the rationalist fallacy that the 'winner' of the struggle over the form of nationalization was that side with the 'best' arguments. Clearly in this case such a view would be totally misleading. Morrison had very poor arguments against the two-tier board but still won. A considerable part of the reason for this was that the unitary board structure had been long established in Britain and any movement to alter that form would have required cutting across a whole set of existing modes of organization with their accompanying legal forms, ideological supports, etc. By contrast, in Germany the advent of worker directors had not required such a radical change because the two-tier board system already existed prior to the revolution of 1919.

Also worthy of note in relation to this particular point of the argument about the public corporation is that socialist arguments about the role of expert management were strongly dependent on points deployed in wholly different arguments. On the one hand there was the idea of the 'managerial revolution' which became popular around this time, especially following the work of James Burnham (1940). On the other hand there was the very general support of rationalization and the necessity of expert management to implement this creating ideologies which have since become known as 'technocratic' (Chester 1952, p. 34). This had always of course been a strong element in Fabian argument but around this time it was apparent in writings across the political spectrum – for example in the Liberal Party's *Britain's Industrial Future* (1928) and later in Macmillan's *The Middle Way* (1938). This is brought out simply to stress that, as noted in the introduction, 'socialist' arguments, however conceived, cannot be treated as if hermetically sealed from non-socialist arguments, and this is a clear instance of the point.

With the pre-eminence of trades unions in British socialist organization, arguments which link the role of unions to the form of nationalization must be accorded considerable weight. One of the central arguments put by supporters of the Morrisonian board was that the alternative of workers' representation would undercut trade union loyalties. If workers' representatives were put on the boards of public corporations, Morrison argued, 'Within a year the Trade Union delegate will be regarded by the rank and file as a man who has gone over to the boss class and cannot be trusted any more' (LP Conference 1932, p. 214). Such representatives would be in a 'contradictory position' (TUC 1931, p. 436), their position would be an anomalous one: if they do not have a majority they will have to take responsibility for unpopular decisions by the boards; therefore the best course is to stay outside (TUC 1932, p. 395). This kind of argument led the TUC in 1944 to argue that trade union personnel *should* go to the boards of public corporations (at the discretion of the minister, and nominated by the TUC) but if they did so they should surrender any position in the union and give up any formal responsibility to that union (TUC 1944, p. 412).

This of course is a very long-standing and crucial argument that always comes up in relation to proposals for industrial democracy –

for example around the Bullock Report, as discussed in Chapter 2. Important to my argument is the need to accept that becoming a board member *will* expose trade unionists to contradictory pressures and criticism. But this position can be seen as the norm of trade union activity rather than an unacceptable deviation. As a delegate at the 1932 Labour Conference put the point, the rank and file would 'say no worse to you on those occasions than they say now' (LP Conference 1932, p. 216). Perhaps even more important is the conception which seems often to lie behind these anti-trade-union-representative arguments, that existing practices of collective bargaining should be largely taken as given. Granted this premise, anything which cuts across those practices has to be seen as simply a 'problem' rather than possibly something itself having favourable consequences.

A good example of this is in the discussion of the London Passenger Transport Board at the 1931 TUC Conference. One supporter of Morrison argued (p. 438) that to have unions on the board of London Transport would necessitate a very large board because of the large number of unions organizing London Transport workers. There is no sense that one of the advantages of board representation might be to open up to questioning such a multiplicity of union representation, that for example the need to co-ordinate board level policy might draw the unions together (again compare the proposal for joint representation committees in the Bullock report).

Existing trade union practices are conceived of not only as largely unproblematic but also essentialized, taken as being what trade unions are really all about. This was commonly done by arguing that these were the issues workers were 'really' interested in. Thus trade unions should only have a role in 'matters that directly and immediately affect labour . . . because it is this kind of control that usually appeals to the worker as being more important and more within his own sphere' (TUC 1933, p. 215), which would exclude consideration of 'technical and commerical policy, sales policy, the raising of finance, the supply of raw material etc.' (ibid., p. 217). A similar line, that workers' main interest was only in their immediate concerns (Morrison 1933, p. 225), was reiterated time and time again. Now it is important not to counterpose to this essentialism an alternative one, that all workers are really keen on controlling their industries if only the unions, etc. did not divert their purpose. The general point at stake here is that the question 'what are workers really interested in?' is a useless way of organizing discussion in this area. The concerns of workers (like all other human agents) are always constructed by a variety of practices which either engage or fail to engage those interests – in this instance this means in particular the practices of trade unions. Trade union practices *are* constrained, but by neither their own essence nor those of their members, rather by all the other contending arguments and practices at the intersection of which they and the worker exist. To put the point more concretely: the ability of trade unions to mobilize workers behind claims for trade union board representation depends on the quality and strength of trade union practices and arguments put forward, and the quality and strength of the contending forces – and little can be said on the outcome of such a struggle without reference to the particular characteristics of such a contest.

In Britain in the 1930s the stress should perhaps be on the general (though certainly not universal) conception within the trade unions of their appropriate activity which largely precluded an aggressive stance on industrial democracy. Constructed on the basis of a sharp dichotomy between the industrial and political spheres, partly predicated on the strength of the doctrine of parliamentary sovereignty, reinforced no doubt by the fragmented structure of British trade unions and above all reliant upon the essentialist notions of workers' 'real' interests sketched above, trade unions were able only to win 'paper' victories on this issue. Thus at the TUC Annual Conference in 1935 a form of words was agreed which bridged the gap between TUC and Labour Party Conference positions by saying that 'the right of workers organisations to be represented on the Governing Boards of socialised industries and services . . . should be secured by statute' (TUC 1935, p. 211). On this exceedingly vague note the trade unions left the matter for almost ten years.

The 'triumph' of the public corporation conception owed a lot to the success of the LPTB (established after the fall of the Labour government in 1931 but in more or less the form proposed by Morrison).[2] This 'success', like any other, is relative to its objectives and therefore can never be unambiguous. But in relation to the objective of providing a co-ordinated, frequent and cheap public transport system the LPTB was undoubtedly successful. Conditions were favourable: competition from cars was trivial, the suburban population was expanding and so providing new sources of revenue. This success made it much more difficult for socialists to argue for alternative objectives, alternative criteria for success, coupled as noted above to the ambivalance (at best) of trade unions towards forms of organization which would cut across their existing practices.

The success of the LPTB also lead to the construction of an argument that its 'precursors', the BBC and Central Electricity Board, were also ideal forms of nationalization. This was an entirely retrospective argument – at the time of their creation they had certainly not been seen in that way (Chester 1952, p. 41). The success of all of these was constantly thrown in the face of those who questioned the equation of the public corporation with 'socialist' industry. Whilst socialist literature in the 1930s did maintain the debate (e.g. Robson 1937; Addison *et al.* 1933), organizationally the public corporation notion swept the board. By 1944 and their 'Interim Report on Post-War Reconstruction' the TUC had accepted it, and by the time of the wave of nationalization after 1945 this form was more or less unproblematic (Morrison 1959, p. 249).

Whilst not wanting to reduce this triumph to the success of a theoretical argument, in conclusion it is worth stressing what can be seen as *the* central theoretical weakness of those who opposed the public corporation. This weakness was one of political theory. Political discussion of the public corporation was dominated by simple notions of interest, their representation and the relation between general and specific interests conceived through the crippling notion of parliamentary sovereignty. As Barry Hindess (1980) observes, the Left had made little advance in this area over the formulations of Rousseau.

NOTES

1 This constraint imposed upon private owners of means of production is one reason why the notions of 'separating from' and 'possession of' the means of production can only be used in a conditional way. This point is taken up again in Chapter 5.

2 Cf. Tivey (1978, pp. 55–6).

CHAPTER FIVE

Revisionism, Marxism
and the
managerial revolution

Revisionism, the criticism of major tenets of existing socialist doctrine, is as old as socialism itself. The revisionism we are concerned with here is however the particular one which erupted on the British Left in the wake of the Labour Party election defeat of 1951 and its recurrence in 1955 and 1959. This revisionism, like all such ideological trends, was over-determined and heterogeneous, it had many different roots and conditions, and the term embraces a set of diverse and not even necessarily compatible positions. Nevertheless there do seem to be certain 'bed-rock' positions which this revisionism argued for, and one of these, a central one, was that there had occurred a 'managerial revolution' which fundamentally altered the character of the capitalist enterprise and capitalism in general and in consequence also the character of socialist politics. (We shall not concern ourselves with other very important aspects of the politics of revisionism, for example its stress on equality as central to socialist ideology. On this see Rose 1980.)

The argument is not that the 'managerial revolution' was necessarily the linchpin of revisionist argument. If we take the work of Crosland and Strachey whose 'contributions were by far the most significant' (Haseler 1969, p. 82), important differences are apparent.[1] Whilst Strachey (1956, p. 35) recognized that 'The management of the decisive units of the economy has become separated from their ownership,' he argued that the crucial feature of the modern corporation was not this, but rather its ability to *affect* prices rather than just take them – because this generated state intervention for or against this price fixing (p. 39).

By contrast, in Crosland's work, which forms perhaps the tablets of stone of post-war revisionism, the idea of the managerial revolution is both central and considered to have very widespread implications. Both these points are summed up concisely by him in his early revisionist piece (Crosland 1952, p. 38):

> Individual property rights no longer constitute the essential basis of economic and social power. Under capitalism, it was the owners of the means of production who were the obvious ruling class. Today, with active ownership converted into passive shareholding, control has passed elsewhere, and much of the traditional socialist-capitalist dispute is irrelevant.

This chapter focuses on the basis of such arguments and on those which were used to oppose them by other socialists. This seems justified not only by the generality of the alleged consequences of the revisionist position, but more particularly because the revisionist debate over the managerial revolution is perhaps the most specific discussion over the nature of the capitalist enterprise yet to have occurred within British socialism.

I

The concept of the managerial revolution was founded upon a prior argument about the divorce of ownership and control in the modern corporation. Whilst earlier expositions of this position can be found, not least in Marx's brief comments in *Capital* (Marx 1972, pp. 436–7), the *locus classicus* of this position is of course Berle and Means, *The Modern Corporation and Private Property* (1932).[2] This book is worth analysing for a moment because of the way some of the problems of the notions of the divorce of ownership and control and of the managerial revolution were present from the beginning.

Centrally Berle and Means argued that the 'corporations have ceased to be merely legal devices through which the private business transactions of individuals may be carried on' (p. 3). The dispersion of shareholdings has meant that these corporations are only in a minority of cases controlled by the shareholders. In 1930, of the top 200 US corporations 65 per cent by number or 70 per cent by wealth were either managerially controlled or controlled by 'legal devices' (pyramiding/non-voting stock) which effectively denied the majority of shareholders any effective control (p. 109).

This separation of ownership from control produces a condition 'where the interests of owner and of ultimate manager may, and often, do diverge' (p. 7). For example the controllers may seek their own profit directly at the expense of the corporation, or indirectly through for example paying labour better than the market dictates (pp. 114–15). In pursuing their own ends the controllers of the enterprise have a great deal of leeway, many of the checks previously imposed by the role of the shareholder having disappeared. The shareholders 'have surrendered all disposition of it to those in control of the enterprise' (p. 9). The separation of ownership and control has 'created economic empires and has delivered these empires into the hands of those who supply the means whereby the new princes may exercise their power' (p. 116). Berle and Means argue even more strongly that the modern corporation 'involves a concentration of power in the economic field comparable to the concentration of religious power in the medieval church, or of political power in the national state' (p. 309).

Starting from this brief outline three major problems of significance to socialist argument on the enterprise can be drawn out. These three problems are only briefly outlined here, to be expanded upon when we look at the way arguments like those of Berle and Means were taken up by revisionism.

The first problem is that of the *divorce* of ownership and control. The conception here is that of two separate groups of individuals, on the one hand shareholders ('the owners') and on the other directors/managers ('the controllers'). The problem with this conception is that it undercuts what seems to be the central point of company law, that the corporation *per se* is a legal personality separate from all individuals. Individuals may be members of the corporation (shareholders) and they may be agents of the corporation (directors) but the corporation is legally separate and irreducible to any individuals (Gower 1979, esp. pp. 97–8). In particular the status of the corporation means that to talk of shareholders owning the corporate assets is a misnomer. 'The corporate property is clearly distinguished from the members' property and members have no direct proprietary rights to the company's property but merely to their shares' (Gower, p. 103). As Lord Justice Evershed put it in a classic judgement in 1948, 'shareholders are not, in the eyes of the law, part owners of the undertaking. The undertaking is something separate from the totality of the shareholdings' (quoted Gower, p. 103).

The implication of this is that to talk of shareholders *as owners* being separated from control is unacceptable. The corporation combines both legal ownership of the assets (with shareholders having very strictly circumscribed rights to intervene in the disposition of those assets) and 'control' of those assets or 'effective possession' in the sense argued for by Cutler *et al.* (1977, 1978). Far from there being a divorce, the marriage of ownership and control is a very close one. The implication of such an argument for the status of the shareholder is clearly radical, but it is one that is in fact hinted at by Berle and Means. They argue that the modern stockholder is so incapable of exercising control of the enterprise that his position is 'in a highly modified sense, not dissimilar in kind from the bondholder or lender of money' (p. 245). And of course no one considers the bondholder or creditor as owner of the corporation. But even here they conceive of this lack of control as an 'economic fact' which the law may tend to reflect over time, but still adhere to the notion of shareholders as currently owners of the corporate assets.

The second problem arises from the notion of *control* of the enterprise. Here again Berle and Means are by no means unaware of the ambiguity of the notion of control. Theoretically, they argue, control of the enterprise 'like sovereignty in the political field, is an elusive concept, for power can rarely be sharply segregated or clearly defined' (p. 66). Practically they get round the problem by locating control with specific individuals with a specific capacity, those individuals 'who have the actual power to select the board of directors' (p. 66). This is in many ways problematic. First it reduces the question of control to that of individual agents, in a similar way to how the question of ownership is reduced to particular individuals (shareholders). This avoids the need to face up to the role of the corporation *qua* corporation. Secondly (and this point is clearly recognized in the quote above about sovereignty) control is unhelpfully conceived as an unconstrained locus of power in general rather than as a capacity to attain particular objectives in particular arenas.

Thirdly the questions of motives arises. Though Berle and Means argue extensively that there had been a divorce of ownership and control in the modern corporation, the implications of this are not addressed at great length by them. Apart from the remarks quoted above about the 'absolutist', etc. nature of management, the question of the practices of management in this situation does not receive serious attention. And in so far as any attention is given, managerial practices are reduced to matters of individual managers, their motives, desires and aims (p. 114). To a large extent this is an amalgam of the two previous problems, a conflation of corporate functions with individuals, and an assumption that there is an unambiguous locus of control in the enterprise – the directors/managers.

These rather abstract arguments and problems fed into the socialist arguments of the 1950s and 1960s, often combined with a rhetoric from another book which played a background role in revisionist formulations about the modern enterprise. This is Burnham's *Managerial Revolution* (1940). Burnham's book properly belongs more to the history of political polemic than to an account of the capitalist enterprise. But it was apparently taken seriously by socialists, even those who were not generally sympathetic to revisionism, for example Crossman (1950, p. 8). 'We went on talking about economic power, and did not notice, until Burnham wrote about it, the growth of managerial society, the separation of ownership from individual power and, equally, the growth of a state apparatus which has a power of its own.'

The central thrust of Burnham's argument was that all societies from about 1914 onwards were undergoing a managerial revolution, which in the end would mean there would be no direct property rights in the means of production. Different countries would go along different routes to this end, but whether through communism, fascism or in democratic countries like the USA, following the coming collapse of capitalism, the trend was towards state ownership of the means of production, with managers controlling these means by their control of the state. The polemical point of the book was a renunciation of Soviet Russia as a 'workers' state', this being the basis of Burnham's renunciation of his previous adherence to Trotskyism. The level of argument of the book may be illustrated from the suggestion (p. 92) that there was no separation of ownership from control because 'ownership *means* control; if there is no control, then there is no ownership'.

The significance of the book was not any profound new arguments it contained but the way in which it could be taken up and used as *one* gloss on the Berle and Means thesis. For the picture Burnham conjured up was one where once divorced from private property, managers would establish a despotism similar to that of Nazi Germany or Stalinist Russia – a far cry even from the 'absolutism' and 'medievalism' suggested as possible by Berle and Means.

II

The quotation from Crosland already given (p. 81) sums up the general way in which the managerial revolution argument was inserted into socialist positions. The explicit enemy being argued against was Marxism, a Marxism which argued 'that the ownership of the means of production . . . imparted to society its essential character' (1974, p. 17). Against this Crosland wanted to argue that capitalists have lost most of the power they once held, partly because of the rise of management independent of capitalists as a consequence of the divorce of ownership from control (1956, Ch. I, esp. pp. 33–5). So 'ownership, while it can influence, does not uniquely *determine* the character of society' (1962, p. 49). Because of this, it has become an anachronism to talk of capitalism at all, and other names have to be thought of (1952, p. 43).

The conception of the divorce of ownership and control has a number of specific implications for Crosland other than serving to refute the Marxist characterization of society. It means that if control of industry is at issue then a change in legal ownership will not suffice. It follows that when talking about nationalization what needs to be questioned is the assumption that because control coincided ultimately with ownership, a compulsory change in ownership was the only way of achieving the end in view. Ownership and control are divorced in the state sector as well as the private so nationalization cannot be the royal road to control (1962, Ch. 3). Similarly, if ownership was divorced from control, ownership by the state could still be pursued but for reasons other than for control. Thus the state might acquire shareholdings in the private sector purely to make sure that some of the financial gains from such holdings accrued to the public rather than private individuals.

In this way the divorce of ownership and control position fed into the current questioning of the centrality of nationalization to socialist politics (see Chapter 4). Crosland made the important point that legal ownership was not the crux of the issue in most cases where socialists were seeking to attain particular objectives in industry. But whilst this may be a pertinent point to make *vis-à-vis* the public sector, its correlate was a range of dubious arguments about the private sector.

Firstly Crosland was not only arguing that ownership was irrelevant to control, but that governments had the means effectively to control private industry without changing ownership. It is perhaps worth spelling out that the second argument in no way logically derives from the first. The argument that ownership may in many cases be irrelevant to control could well go along with an argument that control of private industry in any exhaustive sense is almost *impossible*, that the means to do so would involve such an extraordinary policing operation over an enormous range of loci of decision-making that it seems impossible to conceive outside some totalitarian fantasy world. Yet Crosland argued 'there is now no insuperable *economic* difficulty about the government imposing its will, provided it has one, on either public or private industry. . . . The Government has all the economic power it needs – the only question is whether it chooses to use it' (1956, p. 468). The plausibility of this argument is not improved by the example given to support the thesis that governments can, if they wish, control a privately controlled economy – Nazi Germany. For what is now clear, or should be clear, is that the idea of Nazi Germany as a 'totalitarian' country where every agency obediently followed the dictates of the Führer is grossly to misunderstand what occurred under the Third Reich. Perhaps one of the best-known illustrations of this point is Speer's memoirs (1971) where it is amply shown how *little* control the central authorities in the Nazi state often had over a vast range of other agencies – economic, political and military.

This brings us back to the general way that the managerial revolution argument was taken up by socialists. As we have noted, Berle and Means stressed how the severing of control by shareholders made the modern corporate manager an 'absolutist', and could express against this only the pious hope that 'control of the great corporations should develop into a purely neutral technocracy, balancing a variety of claims by various groups in the community and assigning to each a portion of the income stream on the basis of public policy rather than private cupidity' (p. 312).

Crosland's position on the role of the managers was ambiguous. Where Crossman had endorsed Burnham (1940, p. 8) and suggested that 'the men who run our great industries today form an irresponsible oligarchy' (1952, p. 5), Crosland had explicitly repudiated Burnham-style arguments (1962, pp. 133–4). The divorce of ownership and control, amongst other causes, had brought about a 'change in the psychology and motivation of the top management class itself' (1956, p. 34). Profit has become less important because

> the business leader can also acquire prestige by gaining a reputation as a progressive employer ... or being known to possess high standing in Whitehall ... or by enjoying an outstanding local and civil reputation ... or by displaying obvious patriotism ... or simply by being an intellectual. ... The old-style capitalist was by instinct a tyrant and an autocrat, and cared for no-one's approval. The new-style executive prides himself as being a good committee-man; and subconsciously he longs for the approval of the sociologist. (1956, pp. 36, 38)

This position, which claims to have isolated a radical change in the conduct of management (partly) as a consequence of the divorce of ownership and control, and which makes them seemingly wholly responsive to the public interest, is not adhered to elsewhere. The *Conservative Enemy* (Crosland 1962, pp. 90–1) stresses that the managerial corporations are not really accountable – they are oligarchies which see themselves as quasi-public trustees of the general welfare, but on definitions of welfare they construct themselves. Thus there is a great need for extension of accountability to workers, consumers, local authorities and parliament (1974, p. 42).

This ambiguity seems not to be entirely accidental. If the managerial revolution argument is to serve as a refutation of the Marxist characterization of capitalism then that revolution has to have the consequence of bringing about a major change amounting to a displacement of capitalism. Yet of itself the replacement of one set of individuals (shareholders) by another set (managers) as the controllers of firms has no obvious implication for the way that those firms are conducted. This is especially so if, as Crosland concedes, profits are still very important to these managers. He argues that managers do not profit maximize simply because their own remuneration derives from profits, nor from an altruistic desire to maximize the income of shareholders. Nevertheless the typical controlling manager is interested in high if not maximum profits because his long-term prospects are linked to the growth and profitability of the firm, and in the short-term also because of bonuses and small shareholdings he owns (1956, p. 265). So 'high profits and rapid growth are still the dominant business incentive in Britain' (ibid., p. 266). (There are differences of emphasis if not substance on this point – see for example Crosland 1962, p. 87; Gaitskell 1956, p. 17.)

If this is the case, what difference does the managerial revolution make? Crosland argues that the specific differences are twofold. Firstly he says the managerial controllers will show 'less tenderness' towards the demands of shareholders. Secondly their attitude towards the state will be less hostile towards state intervention than in the days of 'free capitalism' (Crosland 1952, p. 38).

The first of these arguments seems weak. The implication is that manager-controlled firms would be less interested in distributing profits than the old shareholder-controlled type because of the absence amongst the decision-makers of a substantial direct interest in the level of dividends. This makes sense only in the attempted contrast with days when shareholders bled as much out of the firm in the way of dividends as possible and were uninterested in future accumulation. This is surely implausible. The role of profits as both source of immediate income and source of future accumulation always provides a basis for arguments about the appropriate level of distribution, but there is no reason to suppose that this will necessarily be resolved differently between shareholder- and manager-controlled firms. Distribution policy will depend on such things as relative rates of tax on distributed and undistributed profits, taxation of capital gains, policies of competing firms, other sources of finance, etc. (cf. Aaronovitch 1961, pp. 25–9). In particular shareholders may well favour profit retention as a way of maximizing post-tax returns if capital gains are treated more leniently by the tax authorities than dividend income.

Crosland seems to have relied too much on the examples of Sargent Florence (1961, pp. 155–8) who does show that owner-controlled firms in general *do* pay out more dividends in proportion to profits than manager-controlled firms. But this is not supported by other studies (see Nichols 1969; Child 1969, pp. 49–51) and even in Florence the differences whilst significant are not huge and seem an insubstantial group upon which to build a thesis on the disappearance of 'old-style' capitalism. This is especially the case given that by far the most substantial change between pre-war and post-war periods (the period considered by Crosland) was an overall decline in the proportion of profits distributed (Florence, pp. 51–2), a trend general to *all* types of firms.

The second point, a change in attitudes towards state intervention consequent on the growth of managerial-controlled corporations, seems equally insubstantial. The point is not of course to dispute that there was a growth in such intervention after the Second World War but to question whether this had any necessary links with the growth of managerialism. Crosland notes the change in the dominant managerial ideologies after 1945 (e.g. 1956, pp. 33–8) but does not produce any evidence to show the causal relations between this change and the change in control in firms. Certainly with the benefit of hindsight we can argue that this change in managerial ideology was much less permanent than Crosland imagined. This is because it was probably built on much more specific features, for example full employment, relatively rapid growth, strong political pressures, whose disappearance in the 1980s seems to be leading to a reversion to managerial policies reminiscent of Crosland's 'old style' capitalism without any evidence of a reversion to shareholder control in firms. (This lack of causation is more or less conceded by Crosland at one point – 1962, pp. 90–2.)

The general implication then is that Crosland fails to demonstrate that the decline in the role of the individual shareholder in the control of firms has any substantial implications for the way the typical enterprise functions. So that even if one granted that there had been a divorce of ownership from control, revisionism failed to show why this *of itself* should be considered so important as to justify a change in traditional socialist doctrine. (Later work attempting to show clear differences in profit performance between owner and managerially controlled firms is also open to serious objection. For a summary and criticism see Nyman and Silbertson 1978.)

III

As already noted Crosland's arguments were made explicitly against what he conceived of as Marxist and Marxist-inspired positions. The most sustained example of this is in his 1962 book (Ch. 5). His arguments are worth looking at at some length, not because the detailed points are of any great significance, but because the general way *both* sides argue their case seems highly problematic, and takes us back to some of the weaknesses suggested above in the original Berle and Means case.

Crosland accurately argues that the 'New Left' position (as represented by Barratt-Brown 1958 and 1959) has three main thrusts for its attack on the idea of the managerial revolution. Firstly that ownership, particularly institutional ownership, is still sufficiently concentrated to ensure control. Secondly that owner control is re-inforced by an elaborate system of interlocking directorates; thirdly that to the extent that non-owning managers do exercise control, they do so in the interests of the owning class (1962, p. 69).

Crosland argues against all these points. Basing himself again on Florence (1961) he shows that if the criteria are proportion of shares held by director and dispersion of shareholdings, at least two-thirds of the companies in Britain are non-owner-controlled. Secondly that whilst institutional shareholdings are growing the policy of these is to spread their holdings and very rarely to intervene in managerial decisions. He further argues (p. 77) that if in the future (as has been the case) institutions tended to become the majority holder of shares and to use this position to control companies (which has not generally been the case), then this would represent the ultimate divorce of ownership from control. For it is the premium payer and the pension contributor who own these financial institutions but who have ceded control to the managers of the institutions, 'the most extreme example of the divorce between power and property' (ibid.).

Against the second 'New Left' position Crosland argues that the Florence data show that the extent of interlocking directorates is greatly exaggerated. Of the ninety-eight largest industrial companies in Britain, two-thirds had no director or one director in common with any of the 500 largest non-financial companies, the remainder having from two to five (p. 79). Crosland also argues that where there are financed-based directors on industrial company boards these do not play a large part in decision-making, but play the role of part-time 'financial advisers' (ibid).

Finally Crosland contends that the managing groups are from different social strata than the owners and have different relations (control versus ownership) to the means of production (pp. 83–4). Managers have a different attitude both to the level and distribution of profit and to what constitutes a 'responsible' use of economic power (p. 84) (see Section II). Managers the world over are similar in that they all try to maximize income and are subject to the same pressures – technology, large-scale bureaucracy, and the web of rules of the large enterprise. Within this managers bring a variety of motives to bear, though high if not maximum profits in any system will be a substantial concern.

Crosland is possibly right that Barratt-Brown and other Marxist writers have tended to play down the pace with which individual large shareholders have declined in their role as majority shareholders and controllers of companies (e.g. Barratt-Brown 1963, p. 23). But the *pertinence* of the role of such shareholders seems to be taken for granted by both sides. On the one hand revisionists have seen the displacement of such a role as portending fundamental changes in company practices. Marxists on the other hand have commonly argued that capitalism has not changed and have 'sought to convince us that the old time capitalist is alive and well and living in the board room' (Hirst 1979a, p. 127). The similarity in part stems from the original Berle and Means argument for the divorce of ownership and control. For as pointed out such an argument failed to bring out the *combination* of ownership and control located in the corporation *qua* corporation. The corporation was thus always likely to be dissolved into the individuals who allegedly constituted it, whether they be socially conscious managers or profit-grasping capitalists.

Both sides to the revisionist/Marxist dispute thus tended to identify the existence of capitalism with the existence of particular types of *individuals*. For Crosland the decline of '*individual* property rights' (1952, p. 38) was crucial, for those attacking his position a central point was the assertion of the continued role of large shareholders (Barratt-Brown 1963, pp. 23–4); see for later similar positions Miliband 1968; Salaman 1981, p. 165; Crompton and Gubbay 1977, pp. 66–7). The central failing here is the identification of capitalism with the role of certain kinds of individuals rather than a conception of it as a particular form of social relations which at different stages may be supported by different forms of individuality, without losing their character as capitalist (Cutler *et al.* 1977, pp. 273–88, 303–28). This point is discussed further in Section IV.

The question of capital as a social relation is at other points recognized by Marxists. This is in the context of an argument that whatever the other characteristics of managers in firms, they, like 'proper' capitalists, will be driven willy-nilly to maximize profits. Thus Barrett-Brown (1968a, p. 37) argues that boards of directors are not made up of 'managers of technical processes nor managers of labour; but even if they were, we have seen that they must still operate in a system where competition, national and international, can destroy individual companies which fail to pass the test of profitability'. A similar position is argued by Blackburn (1972) and by Westergard and

Resler (1975, Pt III, Ch. 2). Now clearly at one level this is a more substantial argument than one which reduces the operation of the corporation to the motives of individuals. This latter tended to be done not only by Crosland and Berle and Means but also by some Marxists – when for example the latter argue the similar class origins/status, etc. of managers and owners, with the implication that they thereby share the same motives (e.g. Miliband 1968, p. 35). The inadequacy of this position within a Marxist framework is well argued by Poulantzas (1969).[3]

The imposition of profit-maximization by competition is argued by Baran and Sweezy (1968), who generally accept that corporations are managed by self-perpetuating managerial groups who escape share-holder control. They quote Marx's 'Accumulate! Accumulate! That is the Moses and the prophets' but point out that Marx made it clear that this accumulative compulsion arises not from individual pathology but because the capitalist is part of a social mechanism of which he is but one of the cogs. For Baran and Sweezy this social mechanism is still operative, but the urge to accumulate imposed by the profit system applies not to the individual nor to the manager, but to the corporation itself (pp. 53–5).

The progressive nature of such an argument relative to that which reduces profit-seeking to a problem of individual motive should not blind us to its problems. That capitalism involves firms in calculating profits, and that relative profit levels feed into the calculations of financial institutions (stock exchange, insurance companies, banks, etc.) in decisions on financing seem clear enough. But this is not the same as the picture conjured up by some Marxists where it would appear that 'profits' has an unequivocal meaning, independent of its means of calculation; that there is one overseeing site where these profits are calculated; and that any firm falling below some level is simply bankrupted or taken over by another firm. This surely is much too much like the naive neo-classical theory of the firm, a theory which has not only been savaged in a fundamental way by Winter (1964) but which many neo-classical economists would themselves want to maintain a distance from. In particular it conjures up a picture of 'perfect' market mechanisms, which in other contexts (e.g. product and labour markets) Marxists quite rightly want to argue against (see also Chapter 2).

Finally we return to 'control'. As noted above Berle and Means from the beginning of the 'divorce of ownership and control' argument pointed to the equivocal nature of the notion of control as applied to companies. To ask 'who controls?' is an error not only because, as Nichols says (1969, p. 147), such a question assumes an 'oversimplified interpretation of decision making which leads one to equate the manifestation of power with power itself, and to conjure power, authority, and influence' but also because it once again pushes the question back on to the role of individuals, even if these individuals in turn are assumed to represent an interest, as in Barratt-Brown's analysis of the role of bankers on the boards of industrial companies (e.g. Barratt-Brown 1963, p. 26).

The problem of finance is one which can be effectively used to illustrate how questions concerning the 'control' of the company can be helpfully posed *other* than in terms of individuals and their roles. Revisionism (e.g. Crosland 1956, p. 429) pointed out that British industry was to a large extent self-financing, and this was taken to mean that management was largely autonomous from both shareholders and financial institutions in making investment decisions. 'The economic power of the capital market and the finance houses, and hence *capitalist* financial control over industry (in the strict sense of the word), are thus much weaker' (ibid., p. 35).[4]

Against this, Barratt-Brown (1968b, pp. 26–9) attempts to show that the dynamic, fast-growing companies in Britain were heavily (around 50 per cent) dependent on external funds and therefore did not achieve that independence from external financial control alleged by Crosland. (A control which, as already noted, is personified by the important role of financiers and banks on company boards.)

The question of the relation between the level of external financing and the practices of industrial companies is discussed in some detail by Thompson (1977). The great virtue of his article is that he takes on board, and documents, the extent to which British industrial companies are internally financing (p. 253 and Table 1, pp. 254–5), but at the same time shows how this cannot lead to the conclusion that the industrial company is largely autonomous from external financial constraint. On the contrary he argues (p. 265), 'Neither the level of funds that can be retained internally, nor the use to which these can be put is independent of the external constraints under which the units of production work.'

Briefly the argument is that the way internal funds are managed, as represented through such data as earnings ratios, cash flows, liquidity ratios and yield ratios, is 'scrutinized' by finance capital. Such ratios will feed into assessments of the credit-worthiness of the firm and thus its ability to borrow and the terms on which borrowing may take place. In a similar way the earnings of the company will feed into stock exchange assessments of the company. This is not important directly, as the stock exchange is only a trivial source of new funds for most British companies, most of its activity being trading in existing shares. But share prices function as a general index of credit-worthiness, and also may act as signals on the possibilities and likelihood of a takeover of the firm. So even if uninterested in raising funds there, a firm cannot be indifferent to the price of its existing shares.

The point here is not to follow Thompson into a detailed account of the British financial system (important as that is) but to use his arguments to make a general point. This is that the clear implication of his article is that the question of 'control' of enterprises can only be posed through questions concerning, amongst other practices, the conditions of lending and borrowing in the economy. That is, rather than asking 'who controls?' we can perhaps ask 'what controls?', the answer being particular kinds of financial practices (linked to accounting/legal, etc. conditions) which govern the distribution and use of funds in the economy. One might want to question the way Thompson uses the notion of banking/finance *capital* in talking of these practices; this, however carefully used, always tends to imply a subject somewhere who is the originating point of these practices. It is much better perhaps to talk of financial *institutions per se* with no attempt to see these institutions as representative of something else. (Though this does not of course mean it is impossible to argue that the practices of these institutions can be construed as having general *effects*, but that these effects are not simply the result of adequate and successful representation of those interests which may gain advantage from these practices.) Nevertheless his position is clearly superior to that of both revisionism and many previous Marxist arguments. Both of these conjure up a simple scheme where 'control' can more or less be quantified in terms of the proportion of outside funds to be raised by the company, and which lends itself to conceiving control in individual terms – so many non-owning managers, so many industrial capitalists, so many bankers. The clear implication of Thompson's argument is that even if a board of directors is made up entirely of third-generation industrial non-owning managers the practices of the firm may still be to a large extent governed by the practices of the financial system, may be in part 'controlled' by these practices.

The approach of Thompson seems to be both a more radical and a more adequate approach to the question of 'control' of modern enterprise than that of either revisionists or their Marxist opponents. The latter's position has recently been restated and elaborated by Zeitlin (1974) whose arguments have been taken up by British socialism in the work of Francis (1980) and Scott and Hughes (1976). In a more orthodox economic framework many similar points have been made by Nyman and Silbertson (1978).

This recent work has rightly stressed that the question of control of the enterprise cannot be discussed, as it commonly is, using simple indices of proportion of shareholdings held by particular persons, groups of persons or institutions. Secondly, that whilst Berle and Means were right to argue that the modern corporation is not like an idealized form of 'direct democracy', where every shareholder voted on how the business should be run, this is not the same issue as that of the precise locus of control of the enterprise.

However the central problem of this recent work is again precisely the way in which 'control' is conceived. On the one hand this group of writers is well aware of the problems of the concept. Francis (1980, p. 24) for example refers to the notion that control rests exclusively with either one group or another and says, 'This is clearly a gross simplification and in fact in every situation a plurality of interests will be exercising some power and influence over the direction any firm is taking.' Along with this goes a stress on the need to look at the 'specific situation of each corporation' (Scott and Hughes 1976, p. 24), given the complexity of interlocking directorates, the pyramidacy of shares and the (increasing) role of financial institutions[5] in corporate shareholding. But these complexities and diversities are all then undercut by arguing that at the end of the day 'the concrete structure of ownership and intercorporate relationships makes it probable that an identifiable group of proprietary interests will be able to realise their corporate objectives over time, despite resistance' (Zeitlin 1974, p. 1091).

As in so many areas of socialist argument, very interesting empirical material is, in the work cited above, deployed within a very weak conceptual framework. Thus this work clearly undercuts many of the positions of managerialist ideologies like that of Galbraith and the exponents of the 'soulful corporation'. It shows the complexity of

the webs of interconnection between corporate entities, both industrial and financial, in the British economy. But the significance of all
this is rather lost in the framework of control by representatives of
class interests within which the material is deployed.

IV

The central point of this chapter has been to argue that the notions of
the divorce of ownership and control and the managerial revolution
are both unhelpful in the analysis of modern capitalism and the
modern capitalist enterprise. This is *not* to argue that the modern
capitalist enterprise is the same as it has always been, that beneath
the changing phenomenal forms the essence remains the same. The
problem is precisely the nature of this 'essence', against which
changes in the capitalist enterprise may be assessed.

This 'essence' needs to be specified in terms of a form of social
relations, not the existence or otherwise of particular categories of
individuals. These social relations have been defined by Cutler *et al.*
(1977, p. 249) 'in terms of the effective possession of the means of
production by one category of economic agents and the consequent
effective separation of another category of agents' and where the
form of possession and separation takes on a particular character,
for example labour power exists as a commodity.[6]

This seemingly abstract definition has a number of radical consequences in relation to the conceptions of the corporation present in
the 'managerial revolution' debate. First the authors make it absolutely clear that the agents of possession need not be individuals,
but that on the contrary the norm of modern capitalism is that the
corporation *per se* has effective possession.[7] And despite the legal or
customary privilege accorded to human individuals in such discussions, these non-human agents are not reducible to the human agents
who direct them.

Secondly this notion evades the legalism of discussion of the
enterprise which must follow from a focus on questions of ownership.

Thirdly this definition has no truck with the dominant form of
sociological and socialist discussion of the modern corporation, that
which sees the modern corporation as a representation of interests.
Much of the managerial revolution argument can be crudely
summarized as on the one hand the argument that the modern
corporation pursues management interests (which may or may not

coincide with the general interest) and the riposte that in fact by a variety of means the interests of shareholders are still effectively served. Of course it is common in socialist arguments to move from a definition of social relations to the positing of interests as a consequence of those relations, and to talk of these rather than politically constructed interests (see Tomlinson (1981a) for this point in a related context). To talk of the corporation in terms of effective possession or separation from the means of production does not have to imply any interest of the agents in possession (or equally those separated) in attaining any particular objective, including the objective of changing those social relations. This would make it possible to analyse corporate practices 'in their own right' without a constant slippage into conceiving them as representing something else. Such a conception would then evade the severe problems of the notion of 'representation of interests' as a mode of analysing institutional practices whilst still making it possible to talk about general *effects* arising from these practices. It would cut across so much sociological and socialist discussion in which the enterprise appears fundamentally unimportant, simply the site where interests constituted 'elsewhere' play out their conflicts.

Fourthly by focusing on the corporation *qua* corporation, and displacing questions of individual motives or individuals as representatives of interests, such formulations make possible the posing of questions about the capitalist enterprise which are not obstructed by the terms employed in the revisionist/Marxist debate. For example the question of 'control' can then be formulated in ways similar to that about finance in Section III. Control then becomes a matter not of an attribute of particular groups or individuals but a series of practices which construct particular loci of decision-making with particular modes of calculation and thus with a determinate set of possible outcomes. This is *not* to argue, it should be stressed, that some loci of decision-making may not be more important than others, for example company boards of directors more important than the deliberations of a works council. But such a relative importance should not be construed as an unequivocal location of control at the former and its absence at the latter, but rather as the consequence of a series of practices – legal, financial, managerial – which give a broader range of decision-making possibilities to the company board rather than to the works council.

This may seem a semantic quibble, but on the contrary I would argue that such a formulation is crucial if we are to avoid conceiving of the firm as a subject (see Hirst 1979a), self-constitutive and able to realize its objectives. Rather we should see the firm itself as a series of diverse practices, brought together in different ways as a consequence of different calculations engaged in by agents within and without the enterprise, but having no essential unity nor one boundary surrounding it. As an entity with no single point of control, no superordinate authority, but on the contrary as one in which the possessing agency is always trying to co-ordinate diverse and possibly contradictory practices in order to 'keep the show on the road'. What such a conception of the firm might mean for socialist politics in relation to the capitalist enterprise is taken up in Chapter 7.

NOTES

1 A much earlier 'revisionist' text, greatly regarded in the 1950s, was E.F.M. Durbin's *The Politics of Democratic Socialism* (1940). But the central thrust of this text was the centrality of democratic reform for socialist politics, argued very much on psychological grounds, and aimed at communism. The divorce of ownership and control argument is recognized but does not play any major part.
2 For the relation of Berle and Means's argument to Marx, see Hirst (1979a, pp. 127–30).
3 For Crosland's equivocation on the social origins of managers compare his 1952 book (p. 38) where its similarity to the origins of capitalists is asserted, and his 1962 book (p. 83) where it is denied.
4 This is very similar to Baran and Sweezy's argument (1968, p. 29) that because modern industrial corporations raise most funds internally they 'avoid subjection to financial control which was so common in the world of Big Business fifty years ago'.
5 For interesting empirical work on this see also Minns (1980), though this does not escape the problems discussed here concerning the concept of 'control'.
6 For some problems of such a definition see Hindess (1978) and Chapter 7 of this book. In the current context however the notion of 'effective possession' marks an important break with previous socialist conceptions.
7 Cf. Scott (1979, p. 34). Cutler *et al.* contra Scott do *not* argue that 'the enterprise is necessarily the only collective actor capable of effective possession' (see p. 287). Scott (pp. 34–5) also seems to confuse the issue by simultaneously going along with Cutler *et al.*'s definition of the capitalist enterprise, but still talking as if shareholders have legal ownership of the corporate assets.

CHAPTER SIX

The Labour Left: mesoeconomy, monopoly and multinationals

In the 1970s and early 1980s the analysis of modern capitalist enterprises has played a central part in the Labour Left's general approach to and policy proposals for the British economy, formalized as the 'Alternative Economic Strategy' (AES). As with all such debates there is no one book, pamphlet or article which can be said wholly to encapsulate these arguments, but here the focus is on Stuart Holland's *The Socialist Challenge* (Holland 1976) as the most extended and comprehensive statement of this position. Whilst no doubt many of those who broadly support the AES would take issue with particular aspects of Holland's argument, the theoretical assumptions of this argument seem generally accepted by much of the British Left, even by the opponents of the strategy for which these assumptions are used as a support (e.g. Glyn 1978); and support for some of his central propositions comes from surprising quarters (Owen 1981, p. 51). It is strongly present in the important *Labour's Programme 1973*, especially Chapter 2, the Labour election manifesto of 1974, and more recent discussions of the AES such as that by the CSE London Group (1980) or Aaronovitch (1981). Holland's analysis also continues a long if rather thin series of works by British socialists stressing the role of monopoly – for example Aaronovitch (1955; 1961) and in slightly different vein Aaronovitch and Sawyer (1975).

The central thrust of Holland's argument is that the current crisis of capitalism is based on a fundamental change in the structure of capitalist industry and of the enterprises that make up that industry.

The accelerated trend to monopoly and multinational enterprise has resulted in a new 'mesoeconomic' power in between conventional macroeconomics and microeconomics which has 'eroded Keynesian economic policies, and undermined the sovereignty of the capitalist nation state' (Holland 1976, p. 9). So changes in the structure and behaviour of capitalist enterprises are seen as the core of a new phase of capitalism, that new phase 'making imperative' socialist economic policies.

The general character of Holland's argument has a great deal in common with the long-standing orthodox Marxist notion of monopoly capitalism (albeit with some new terminological twists). In both cases changes in the structure of capitalist enterprises are seen as having such widespread effects on the economy as to justify talking about a wholly new era in capitalism. In both cases the notion of monopoly and the contrast implied with a non-monopolistic, competitive past is the fulcrum of the analysis.

As has already been argued in Chapter 1 the Marxist conception of monopoly capitalism is an extremely problematic one, which is either largely unrelated to Marxist concepts of the economy, or where more closely specified depends on dubious presuppositions as to the centrality of changes in the size of the enterprise. Because of the parallel between Holland's 'mesoeconomy' and the Marxist notion of 'monopoly capitalism' much of the general argument in Chapter 1 concerning the Marxist position would be applicable to Holland. But those arguments will not be repeated here. Instead this chapter will take up the more specific arguments of Holland relating to the *effects* of monopoly. Following this his arguments relating to multinationals will be similarly assessed.

I

For Holland the crucial index of monopoly is the concentration of production in fewer and fewer large firms. The central evidence of a move towards the monopolistic mesoeconomy is therefore data on the concentration of industry, the proportion of total manufacturing output produced by the 100 largest companies. Holland cites Prais (1974) as showing that this share has arisen form 16 per cent to 42 per cent in 1968, a probable 45 per cent in 1970, and with a projection of two-thirds by the mid-1980s.

A number of preliminary points can be made on these figures.

Firstly there is the question of the status of these percentages. The trend is much less clear-cut than Holland's presentation would suggest. Prais himself has revised down the figures (in Prais (1976) – published of course after Holland). In particular his figure for 1970 was revised down from the 45 per cent of his 1974 paper to 40–1 per cent in the 1976 book. This in turn undercuts the projection of two-thirds by the mid-1980s. Secondly the method of calculating such percentages is fraught with considerable problems. Slightly different methods can produce different results. For example official (HMSO 1976) data give figures of 36 per cent for 1963, 39 per cent for 1968, 38 per cent for 1970, and 39 per cent for 1971. More importantly even if we take Prais's figures as of 1976 these seem a weak basis on which to build arguments about long-term trends. He admits (1976, p. 4) that the 1909 and 1924 figures are 'approximate' and should be treated with special reserve. Given this and the point that Holland's argument is solely concerned with the post-1945 period, we can reasonably take just the figures since 1945, which are as follows (Table 1).

TABLE 1 Share of 100 largest firms in manufacturing (net output)

	%
1949	22
1953	27
1958	32
1963	37
1968	41
1970	38

Source: Prais (1976, p. 4)

These figures would seem to suggest a strong upward movement between 1949 and the early 1960s which has since slowed down and may have halted. This is a far cry from the image of a runaway, accelerating process conjured up by Holland.

Secondly as an index of concentrated 'economic power' they have to be qualified by the fact that they refer only to *manufacturing* industry whose share of total domestic output is around 33–7 per cent. The centrality commonly given to manufacturing in studies of industrial concentration partly reflects an implicit assumption that it is manufacturing which is 'vital' to the economy. Now it may well be that the size and efficiency of the manufacturing sector is vital for specific economic policy objectives (see e.g. Singh 1977). But if the concern is (as with Holland) almost the whole range of economic objectives it is not at all clear that manufacturing occupies a central place in relation to all of these. For example in relation to employment, manufacturing employs a slightly smaller share of the total labour force than its share of output; why should the structure of this minority sector of around 30 per cent of employment then be given such a central role in determining the success of overall policy? Such centrality may perhaps be justified but Holland nowhere argues this.

The third general problem relates to the implications of concentration for monopoly, that is how far the process of concentration has undercut the existence of competition. The existence or otherwise of competition can either be evidenced by direct implication from the structures of production or indirectly be registered by relative prices, relative profits or other indices of 'performance'. This latter kind of argument is taken up in Section II.

An initial point that must be made on the first area of argument is that there is a general problem of inferring anything about competition from industrial *output* as competition must always presumably relate to a market. Orthodox economic theory defines markets in terms of cross elasticities of substitution between products – where such elasticities are 'high' then market competition can be said to exist. This raises the problem of what 'high' in this context means and also the question of the time period considered to be relevant to the calculation.

But additional to the theoretical vagueness of general definitions of markets there is a much more serious point, that the data used in industrial studies are not the product of the theoretical concerns of economists but of a range of 'administrative' exigencies. This means that industries are grouped largely on 'supply side' rather than 'demand side' characteristics. Agencies compiling such figures are bound to use definitions which are practicable, that is generate clear-cut data. This often requires the researcher to follow the way the industries themselves or trade associations group and classify production. There is thus a *radical* incompatibility between the standard definitions of industrial production and the definitions which would

102

flow from the use of economists' criteria (see Scherer 1980, pp. 59–64).

In addition to this general problem, if one wanted to infer anything about competition in Britain from the structure of production, account must be taken of imports, that is how far the concentrated nature of domestic production is undercut by foreign competition. Such figures are not to my knowledge available, and to compile them would undoubtedly raise severe computational problems, for example in matching domestic output to appropriate categories of imports. Given however the large increase in production of manufacturing imports in the UK in recent years this qualification would seem likely to be a significant one.

Secondly Holland's analysis of industrial competition treats *legal* units as central to that process. The process of creating larger and larger legal units (enterprises) which replace a large number of previous small companies is seen as a straightforward sign of the demise of competition. But this does not follow. Firstly as Holland well recognizes (p. 51) the typical 'top 100' firm is a diversified, multi-product entity. So in any one product market the number of competing products may be wholly unaffected by a movement from a low to a high overall concentration ratio. For example in Table 2

TABLE 2

Products	Enterprises		
A	X	Y	Z
B	X^1	Y^1	Z^1
C	X^2	Y^2	Z^2
D	X^3	Y^3	Z^3

initially there are four products, each produced by three firms, making twelve separate sites of production in all. Assuming equality of product output and firm size the concentration level is such that the top three firms produce 25 per cent of total output. If there is then a wave of takeovers with X taking over X^1, X^2, X^3 and Y taking over Y^1, Y^2, Y^3, Z taking over Z^1, Z^2, Z^3, the concentration ratio is then such that the top three firms have 100 per cent of output. But the implications for competition in any one product market are in principle zero, as each still has three firms competing within it. Of course this is a highly simplified example, but the point is that given the generality of multi-product enterprises, overall concentration ratios by themselves can tell us nothing about the structure of possible competition in any one product area. There is in Holland a slippage between stressing the oligopolistic nature of most markets (1976, p. 44) but citing evidence mainly relating to overall concentration (e.g. pp. 49–50).

Secondly multi-divisional organization means that to a greater or lesser degree different product-producing units are autonomous from the central control of the enterprise. Holland (1976, p. 51) cites the case where 'apparently competitive' products are, unbeknown to consumers, sold by the same firm. However, why this form of competition should be considered only 'apparent' is not clear. Depending on the different marketing strategies of the divisions involved, these products may be 'genuinely' competing in the sense that each division is trying to increase its share of the market by pricing, advertising and other sales policies. Holland assumes that because at one level there is a legal (and hence financial) unification of the firm, the autonomy of the parts of the firm is wholly illusory. But this is not justified. The autonomy of such parts may be limited and constrained for example by the company's overall financial strategy, but within the areas it is allowed to operate there is no reason why it should be considered less effective than competition between legally separate entities. Holland here seems to make that common con-flation in socialist discussions of the enterprise of talking about legal entities, 'capitals', as if they 'really' are units of control of production, and organizational divisions within these legal entities as serving merely to obscure that reality.

Holland's discussion of industrial structure and its implications for competition can in some respects be turned on its head. Thus Clifton (1977) has argued that the institutional conditions for mobility of capital and therefore effective competition amongst firms are much more readily attained by the modern multi-product giant firms than by the small single-product firms of the past. 'It is the range of competitive strategies available to the large firm and the intensity with which they may be applied to the market in the search for competitive advantage that makes the contemporary capitalist economy dominated by such firms far more competitive than ever before' (p. 149). Large firms with knowledge and resources across a range of different industries are in a much better position to compete with other firms than smaller firms whose resources are small and tied to a particular product. Whilst this competition is seen as 'oriented around investment behaviour and not market behaviour *per se*' (p. 149), nevertheless market competition is a crucial means by which the competition between these large units of capital is fought out. Of course this market competition does not necessarily take the form of price competition (a point taken up further below) – this is but one of several strategies available alongside product innovation, diversification, mergers, etc. The multiplicity 'gives the firm added flexibility in responding to changes in market conditions and in initiating them. In short, it means that the large firm is far more competitive' (p. 148).

The general point to be stressed is that even if the data on concentration in manufacturing showed an unambiguous upward trend, the implications of this for competition are at best unclear. Holland when talking of competition and monopoly is unambiguously talking about 'market power' (1976, Chapter 2) and yet this implies an analysis of markets which is not provided either on an aggregate ('the British market') or individual product level. The example he quotes of the capacity of big firms to take advantage of monopoly (the Swiss drug company Hoffman La Roche) seems doubly inappropriate. Firstly of course this company would not figure in British output as opposed to the British market so concentration ratios are wholly irrelevant. Secondly it is clear that the extortionate profiteering of this company was dependent on such elements as patent protection which can only be discussed at the level of particular product markets, precisely the level of analysis foresworn by Holland.

II

These general criticisms of Holland can be supported in discussing the more specific ways in which he argues the mesoeconomy undercuts the pursuit of policy goals by governments. The first area is that of prices. Price levels and price movements are seen by Holland both as indices of the presence/absence of competition and as a means by which mesoeconomic firms are able to obtain high profits. To take the first point. The assumption that prices can be largely deduced from industrial structure is central to a major strand in neo-classical economics, which is always inclined to exaggerate the passivity of firms in relation to 'the market', instead of seeing firms as having various strategies both to adapt to and to change the market. Therefore even where evidence is adduced relating to industrial structure in one particular market (as opposed to the manufacturing sector as a whole, as in Holland), pricing *policy* should not be seen as merely reflecting this, but as being much more active. This is stressed by Eichner (1976), where although oligopoly is taken as the normal environment of firms' pricing decisions, this can only be the starting point for a much more complex elaboration of the forces entering into price determination. Holland offers only fleeting accounts of the likely pricing policies of mesoeconomic firms. For example on p. 53 the large firm is presented pushing up prices in a way unavailable to the small, competitive firms, whereas on p. 59 the mesoeconomic firm is pictured as commonly providing a 'price umbrella' for small firms so that these latter do not complain to regulatory authorities about the practices of mesoeconomic firms. These particular points are made simply to stress the unsound basis of any argument that attempts to deduce any simple notion of pricing behaviour from the size of firms and/or the structure of the market.

Attempts to link market concentration and price should thus be treated sceptically, both on *a priori* grounds and because attempts to establish such relationships empirically are fraught with disabling problems, above all problems of identification, that is isolating the effectiveness of one variable. On this latter point see for example Phillips (1976).

Equally pricing behaviour cannot be used as an index of the existence of competition *per se*. Pricing policy is, as Holland acknowledges (1976, p. 53), only one aspect of competition, there are a variety of other ways that big firms may and do compete (advertising, better after-sales service, etc.). In addition it is acknowledged (p. 61) that the scale of resources available to large firms may be a necessary condition for price competition, where existing firms establish barriers to entering the market (by for example heavy advertising) which no small firm has the resources to penetrate.

This implies that the central problem of what Holland calls the 'competitive model' of the firm's behaviour may be more its stress on the particular forms of competition rather than the existence of competition *per se*. However there is a danger, which Holland and other socialist economists do not always avoid, in erecting a straw man in characterizing the price theory of orthodox economics the more easily to ridicule it. Thus Holland generally derides the role of demand in determining prices, stressing the capacity of the firm to override the dictates of consumer demand. Certainly it clearly seems to be the case that 'naive' neo-classical arguments are implausible in suggesting a rapid adjustment of prices to market conditions, implying that most commodities are sold on an auction basis, that is with no price attached before entering the market. But more sophisticated orthodox accounts recognize that pricing decisions are normally initially based on some version of cost-plus, but that adjustment to market trends takes place when for example order books shorten, inventories rise and *ad hoc* pricing adjustments or perhaps changes in quality take place in response (e.g. Hay and Morris 1980, pp. 135–9). The argument here is not that such accounts are adequate, and Coutts, Godley and Nordhaus (1978) for example suggest that they are not, but that too much political argument about pricing policy takes place with caricatured positions so that these arguments always 'slide past' one another rather than confronting directly.

As to the effect of mesoeconomic power on the general price level, in particular on inflation, this also is much less clear than Holland's argument suggests. Firstly the only evidence cited for this relationship (1976, p. 62) relates to American material showing econometrically established relationships between market share and high prices. But leaving aside the severe methodological problems of such studies, they in any case relate to a static one-off position, not to a *process* of inflation which must imply price behaviour over a period. The central point, 'A correlation between the trend to monopoly in the main economies of the capitalist system and the accelerating inflation' (p. 61), is not at all directly established. Impressionistically such a correlation would appear implausible. As Holland's own figures show, the great acceleration in concentration took place in the 1960s in Britain, whilst the great period of rapid inflation began in the early 1970s when the concentration boom 'had subsided'. Equally the countries with most rapid inflation rates in the world in recent years (e.g. Argentina, Israel) do not appear to have very highly con- centrated industry, nor do low inflation countries (e.g. Switzerland, West Germany) have notably low levels of industrial concentration. Holland's argument appears to be an extreme case of a crude cost- push notion of inflation which implausibly ignores the role of differing macroeconomic conditions in different countries, different exchange rate regimes, etc. in generating differential rates of inflation. The most careful recent British work argues that there is no evidence that 'extremely high levels of, or extremely high increases in, concentration are associated with faster increases in prices' (Hart and Clarke 1980, p. 80).

Holland (1976, p. 64) suggests that inflationary pricing policies by mesoeconomic firms are self-defeating because they eventually lead to consumer resistance and foregone sales and output. Yet such a story implies grossly naive policies on behalf of mesoeconomic firms, a *reductio ad absurdum* of cost-plus pricing policy, where declines in demand simply affect the firm's level of output and prices are completely unchanged. Mesoeconomic firms surely cannot be both the conniving, calculating entities as conjured up elsewhere by Holland and at the same time so thickheaded as to be willing to commit financial suicide in this manner.

As a consequence of their capacity to employ cost-saving techniques, but especially by virtue of their price-fixing abilities, Holland suggests that mesoeconomic firms are able to earn profits 'which are greater than the "norm" earned in the remaining competitive sector' (p. 53). His analysis, as he says (p. 54), assumes that big firms in general make bigger profits than smaller firms. Two linked points on this assumption are worth stressing. First, here as elsewhere there is a conflation of size and concentration. Big firms may for example make higher profits than small firms even where there exists very severe competition because of 'economies of scale' in the broadest sense (a point returned to below). Secondly there is econometric evidence of a small but significant relationship between *concentration* and profitability, but again this is open to severe qualification.[1] The correlation is most robust where substantial barriers to entry exist – precisely, as suggested, something which the growth of mesoeconomic firms may make *less* effective. In addition the correlation is just that – the problem of identification of *causal* connections is severe. As Phillips (1976, p. 248) stresses, 'market concentration may be the cause of high profits, or conversely market concentration and high profits may be the result of superior performance by a few firms'.

Overall the conclusion of the recent work by Hart and Clarke (1980, p. 82) seems appropriate.

No doubt examples of a positive effect of concentration on profitability in some industries can be found but there are always

108

equivalent counter examples. It is unlikely that any large representative sample of industries will reveal a general association between profitability and concentration because the relationship between economic performance and market structure is very complex.

Holland argues that mesoeconomic companies' real profit levels will be disguised – the declaration of profits is managed by the firm in order not to invite unwanted attention by government authorities. Accounting standards are sufficiently elastic for firms to be able to make their declaration fit in with their desires. This is an important point, and it can well be argued that there is a good case for much more regulation of accounting standards in the UK (see G. Thompson 1978). But Holland's point is not mainly this, it is that differential profit levels between mesoeconomic and other firms are disguised by accounting practices. But why should this capacity to 'manage' declarations apply only to these large firms? Indeed Holland himself (p. 57) admits that 'even in small companies, an accountant can ask annually whether management wants to declare a profit, a break-even or a loss'. The *multinational* status of large firms may affect their capacity to control profit declarations, but Holland signally fails to establish that there is a substantial difference in this regard between large and small firms, and that there are grounds for believing that large firms' behaviour in areas regulated by state agencies is in many ways *better* than small firms (because there are fewer to regulate). Take for example the widespread evasion by small firms of wage council determined levels of minimum wages (Winyard 1976).

A problem which arises in talking of high mesoeconomic profits in Britain is that if these firms are also held to dominate manufacturing activity then this sector as a whole would be profitable, indeed with increasing concentration it should be increasingly profitable. But this is surely wholly implausible. Whatever the exaggerations which may have been made in the 1970s period about declining company profitability (Holland, pp. 57–8) and notwithstanding the severe calculative problems, the long-term trend seems undeniable, a declining level of profits with levels below those of other national economies (e.g. Glyn and Sutcliffe 1972; Williams 1979). Not only is there a general low level of profits, but this is most marked in manufacturing (especially if chemicals are excluded), where industrial concentration is much the most significant and where all the focus of Holland's book is.

This picture cannot be readily denied by invoking the malleability of company accounts because it is based on national accounts data as well as company accounts, and indeed company accounts in recent years have shown consistently higher rates of return than the 'real' rate, particularly because of the still widespread use of historic cost accounting. This last point also suggests that while it is appropriate to consider accounting practices as other than a simple *representation* of magnitudes which exist independently in the real world, the conventions they embody are not simply the emanations of capitalist interests. Otherwise, for example, historic cost accounting would presumably have been abandoned by capitalist firms long ago, as declaring high (because non-inflation adjusted) profits seems hardly to favour capitalist interests in for example the conduct of wage negotiations.

To put the general point another way. The high and increasing levels of concentration in British manufacturing industry, if this is a correct picture, have not prevented profitability in this sector from declining almost continuously. These levels of profit reflect much more deep-seated practices – managerial, cultural, work organizational, etc. – and are relatively impervious to industrial structure. Rather than mesoeconomic firms earning high profits against the wish of UK governments, the recent pattern has been of largely cosmetic price controls combined with substantial tax concessions by governments aimed to cushion the effects of declining pre-tax profits on post-tax outcomes.

Apart from prices and profits, Holland suggests that mesoeconomic firms have also undercut other government objectives, notably in such areas as investment, trade, pricing, job creation and regional development (1976, p. 30). In none of these cases are the mechanisms of this frustration spelt out as consequences of industrial concentration *per se*. They may be linked to the questions of multinational enterprises but that is in principle a different point from levels of concentration of domestic industry (see p. 112ff.). More important in general is Holland's conflation of the two questions of the obstructive role of big firms and the problems of governments successfully pursuing objectives constrained by the existence of a largely privately owned economy. That is to say Holland implies an exaggerated view of the ability of governments in capitalist economies to achieve their objectives *regardless* of the nature of the industrial structure. For example his argument on employment is that up to some date in the

1960s Keynesian policies could and did generate full employment, but that this was undermined by the growth of the new mesoeconomic mode of production (e.g. Holland, p. 14). But this story exaggerates the role of government in generating this post-war period of full employment which owed more to the high levels of private investment and the dynamism of world trade than any direct effect of government policy (see Matthews 1968; Tomlinson 1981b; Tomlinson 1981c, especially Ch. 8). Equally the failure of British governments to raise the level of manufacturing investment or productivity to the levels of major trade competitors has persisted through all the policy changes and all the changes in industrial structure of the post-war period. In this respect as in others it would seem that Holland has failed to establish that the rise in industrial concentration in manufacturing has fundamentally altered the economic process in Britain – governments *never had* the kind of capacity to determine economic policy which Holland's argument states was undermined by the rise of mesoeconomic power.

A final point on Holland's 'mesoeconomic' thesis relates to his account of the reasons for increasing concentration. Despite his many barbs aimed at orthodox neo-classical economics, Holland's account of these reasons is extremely orthodox. Above all he stresses the role of technological economies of scale which favour the growth of large firms. This perhaps is amenable to socialists as it has authority in Marx, from whom Holland himself quotes (1976, p. 52). As already noted in Chapter 1 this is only one aspect of Marx's account of the process of centralization and concentration. Marx also stressed the role of financing in favouring the large firms, and this is of course the main thrust of Hilferding's orthodox Marxist argument, an author cited approvingly by Holland on other points. The importance of this point is twofold. First those accounts which give a central role to financing in the growth of industrial concentration in Britain appear more adequate than those which stress the role of 'economies of scale' in a narrow technological sense. For example the arguments of Prais (1976) appear convincing in this area. Politically more significant, such accounts problematize the evolutionary/inevitability aspect of the Holland-style argument which sees growing concentration as inescapable under private capitalism because it is based on continuous growth of technological economies of scale. In this way the 'socialist challenge' has the force of an imperative; only socialism can deal with the consequences of this ineluctable process (e.g. Holland 1976, p. 9). This seems dangerous ground for socialist politics. Socialists have invested too much already in prognoses of the inevitability of socialism to the detriment of analyses of the political forces necessary for such a movement. Holland's arguments provide no better ground than any others for accepting the force of this inevitability, conceptual and empirical implausibility compounding political wishful thinking.

III

The argument of the Labour Left is that the characteristic company of the new phase of capitalism is not only mesoeconomic but also multinational. The mesoeconomic firm undercuts government policy because it is no longer the small and weak microeconomic company bowing to the wishes of powerful government. The multinational company undercuts government's capacity to pursue major economic policies by its ability to switch resources from one country to another within itself and on its own terms and thus to subvert common mechanisms of economic policy established on the basis of predominantly national firms. Whilst mesoeconomic and multinational firms may in practice be the same (all the top 100 manufacturing firms in Britain are multinational), in principle the analysis of the effects of these multinational firms can be separated from that of the domestic mesoeconomic firm.

The purpose of the argument in this section is not to argue that the claims commonly made about multinational companies are wholly illusory and that they raise no problems for the pursuit of national economic policies, socialist or otherwise. Rather the argument is that in several respects the way in which multinationals are discussed by the Left is inadequate and that a major effect of this inadequacy is to exaggerate the degree to which the growth in size of multinationals fundamentally alters the conditions for pursuing economic policies (socialist or otherwise).

First there is the general way that the effect of multinationals is conceived in terms of loss of sovereignty on the part of national governments. (In addition to Holland 1976 see Kennett, Whitty and Holland 1971 and Labour Party 1977.) If this loss of sovereignty simply implied an unfavourable change in the conditions under which economic policy is pursued it would be unobjectionable. But it is charged with other elements. The arguments over loss of sovereignty due to the rise of multinationals is part of a general political theory popular on the Left and is notably parallel to that of the Labour Left concerning Britain's membership of the EEC. What is at stake in such arguments is a loss of sovereignty by the *national parliament* to other bodies. The argument thus is strongly constitutionalist – the British constitution makes parliament sovereign and this status for parliament is both desirable and possible if the EEC and multinationals do not derogate from parliament's powers.

Such an argument, whether in relation to the EEC or multinationals, is objectionable on a number of grounds. Firstly such a doctrine must always be problematic for democratic socialists as it implies a degree of perfection in the democratic status of parliament which seems wholly out of touch with the depth and range of criticisms of parliament which can and are made by socialists on other occasions. Such unproblematic support for parliament seems to be complicit with the quaintly anachronistic flavour of much Labour Party left-wing rhetoric which would see the Putney Debates and *Gulliver's Travels* as the high points of political argument. Yet the pressing problem for socialists today would seem to be to attack and reform the many and manifest shortcomings of parliament, and to do this not in the name of some return to a pristine state but in the name of abolishing many entrenched parliamentary traditions which function as obstacles to a more accountable legislature and executive.

The corollary of this first point is that such constitutionalist arguments gravely exaggerate the effective capacity of parliament *prior to* either entry to the EEC or the growth of multinationals. Thus much argument against EEC membership was based on the belief that the capacity of a socialist majority in the UK parliament to achieve socialism would be fatally hindered by the powers of the Brussels bureaucracy. Such a view (leaving aside the enormous optimism in the belief in an impending socialist majority) greatly understates the wholly domestic obstacles such a majority would face – in the civil service, the judiciary, local government, as well as of course from the owners and controllers of private means of production. Similarly arguments that multinationals fatally impair the pursuit of certain kinds of economic policy understate the obstacles to the pursuit of many policies *prior* to the growth of multinationals. (In this respect British socialists may be said to have made too much of a concession to social democrats like Crosland who greatly exaggerated the capacity of post-war governments to determine the practices of private firms in the 1950s and 1960s.)

For example Holland (1976, pp. 64–5, 87–9) argues that the growth of such companies has severely qualified the effectiveness of changes in the pound's exchange rate as a means of improving the UK's balance of payments position. Multinationals do not favour the changes in price competitiveness aimed for by devaluations; they also tend to divide up markets and be unwilling to rearrange such divisions at the whim of governments. In addition multinational companies as dealers in currencies are able to speculate in those currencies which in turn may make devaluations either more likely or more substantial than they might otherwise have been. All of these points have some force, and certainly the stress on the role of international firms in foreign exchange dealing is a useful corrective to those who see currency devaluation as a major and readily available policy weapon (Fishman 1980). However there is ample evidence that *all firms*, multinational or otherwise, do not simply act passively in the face of devaluation. Depending on their calculations as to the appropriate marketing strategy, firms may well see devaluation as an opportunity not to increase sales but to increase profits, and so increase their sterling prices to offset the foreign price implications of the devaluation (Holmes 1978). The point here is that in any economy where enterprises have autonomy in price-setting (whether those enterprises be private or not) a macroeconomic policy such as devaluation may well be to a greater or lesser extent ineffective.

A similar point can be made about research activity. The Labour Party document on multinationals (Labour Party 1977, pp. 32–3) for example argues that these companies do very little basic research. But the central point made to substantiate this criticism is that those companies will only invest in R and D where profit prospects are good. But this point is obviously applicable to all private investment in research activities. As the document effectively concedes (p. 33) the 'British problem' is a combination of low total R and D by all companies and the misdirection of much government-funded research into non-commercial areas like aerospace. The problem has little to do with the role of multinationals, especially in a country like Britain which is the second biggest 'home' of multinationals as well as a site of foreign-owned multinational operations.

The argument in many ways is a banal one, governments in such

114

economies don't directly set prices so they cannot simply order a change in those prices. But the implication is important, that in looking at policy and the constraints on policy the focus should be on those agencies which actually take particular decisions. This is perhaps just another way of saying what has been already said in the discussion of mesoeconomic firms, that Holland and other socialists consistently exaggerate the capacities of government in economic policy *before* the rise of mesoeconomic/multinational firms, thus greatly overstating the changes brought about by that rise.

The loss of sovereignty argument concerns a loss allegedly sustained by a *national* parliament. Here the anti-EEC and anti-multinational arguments come together again – both sets of institutions derogate from the powers of the only legitimate governmental power, that of the UK parliament. Yet clearly the status of these two underminers of Westminster's prerogatives is very different. The EEC has become a governmental agency with an elected parliament based on universal suffrage within the Ten. In principle therefore it would seem to have an equivalent democratic legitimacy to the national parliaments of the Ten. Clearly therefore it is wholly different from the non-democratic (in any sense of that word) multinationals.

Much more than this: the EEC would seem to be precisely a governmental agency which, because of its own 'multinational' status, is likely to be an important weapon in attempting to make effectively accountable and control the operations of multinational companies. This line of argument has been avoided by the Labour Left by two strategies. One line is to argue that in principle the EEC is incapable of performing such a role because this would require both unanimity amongst the Ten's national governments and would 'be in the teeth of the market philosophy of the treaty of Rome' (Labour Party 1977, p. 70). The first of these points assumes that the European parliament will always remain a 'talking shop' with no independent powers of its own to pressurize the national governments. Of course the Labour Left's position on the EEC parliament elections of 1979 seemed designed to make this true, to preserve an ineffective parliament by denying its democratic legitimacy. But this position is by no means inherent in EEC arrangements, the European parliament could be a very powerful channel for the creation of a policy on multinationals. The second argument is more clearly absurd. With this argument legalistic analyses of politics surely reached a *reductio ad absurdum*. The Treaty of Rome was not brought down on tablets of

115

stone, and whatever free market philosophy it may enshrine this has not prevented the EEC from promulgating regulatory and interventionist policies in a whole number of areas. Thus for example the 1980 agreements on controlling steel output in the Ten, rather than letting market forces drive down prices with a probable eventual widespread closure of steel-making capacity. One of the tragedies of the Left's position on the EEC was that by its abstentionist/lukewarm attitude to the European parliament elections it made an EEC commitment to market forces *more* likely by giving conservative political forces the dominant say in that parliament.

Stuart Holland's arguments on the EEC have not been of this kind. He accepts the importance of a 'regional grouping of international states to increase joint surveillance of the terms on which multinationals operate' (1976, p. 78). Equally he has had no truck with the reverence paid to the Treaty of Rome as the determining cause of everything that has happened in the EEC. As he argued (Kennet, Whitty and Holland 1971, p. 27) the community in practice 'has increasingly evolved towards an economic policy recognizably closer to that of the last Labour government and the present Labour Party than to either 19th century liberalism or the neo-Liberalism of the present (i.e. Heath) government'. His argument is simply (p. 79) that *so far* the capacity of the EEC to control multinationals has been disappointing – the blueprints for action have proved unacceptable to either the commission or a member country. This clearly has some weight, but it should be stressed that with all its shortcomings the EEC is one of the few agencies where some measure of control of multinationals is possible. The Left should therefore be aiming to strengthen the role of this agency rather than attacking its legitimacy or stressing only the problems in pursuing such an end. More importantly the notion of sovereignty should be much more critically assessed, whether it be in talking about the EEC or multinational companies.

IV

The second major weakness in the Holland/Labour Left argument on multinationals is an exaggeration of the capacities of these companies to attain their ends, ends which are inimical to national economic policy goals.

Central to the bargaining position of multinationals is their ability to move investment funds relatively easily from one country to another, with all the possible consequences for employment, the balance of payments, etc. Yet this ability should not be overstated. As far as investment in manufacturing capacity goes this is by definition investment in highly specific assets whose value to the multinational concerned is generally very much greater as part of a going concern than as plant to be broken up and sold. The 'golden rule' of economics – that bygones are never bygones – applies to multinationals as it does to all other firms. Once committed to a certain production location, movement elsewhere is not a cheap or easily arrived at decision. The process of disinvestment is, as the Labour Party document recognizes (Labour Party 1977, p. 37) 'often a creeping process, the accumulation of several decisions taken in several ways' and whilst this is obviously still a serious problem it is not the same as if the common pattern were one where companies were 'running away' overnight. The gradual change at least implies some space for processes of negotiation and the application of leverage. Examples can be found of companies which do suddenly close production facilities, but the fact that it is so often the same example which is quoted (Remington-Rand's withdrawal from France in 1962 being the favourite) suggests this is an exceptional rather than common occurence. It is because of this general qualification to the mobility of investment that trades unions have not *in general* found bargaining with multinationals to be that much more disadvantageous than bargaining with domestic firms. 'In practice the day-to-day effects have been considerably less than drastic' (Labour Party 1977, p. 38).

The activities of multinationals are not only constrained by the exigencies of operating with fixed capital. They are also constrained by their own organizational structure. Multinational companies have a variety of different systems of organization – international division structures, global functional structures, etc. (see e.g. Channon and Jalland 1979, Ch. 2; Williamson 1975). All of these structures involve particular patterns of command and decision-making none of which can be reduced to an unproblematic hierarchy where those at the apex of the organization transmit orders and those below obey. Decision-making is necessarily conditioned by the information flows within the organization, the unavoidable if variable degrees of autonomy to lower echelons involved in any organization, these points together meaning that the loci of decision-making is always ambiguous and conditional. This of course means that the formal structure of decision-making may not reflect the underlying patterns of influence within the enterprise (Vernon 1977, p. 29). Organizations, including multinationals, are never simply totalitarian chains subject to the omniscient and omnipotent will of a leader or leaders. For example a multinational company deciding whether or not to close operations in one country will be dependent on, amongst other things, necessarily speculative calculations of relative profitability, dependent in turn on calculations of potential markets, labour costs, industrial relations, etc. In these calculations the central directing body will be dependent to a greater or lesser extent on information from the country concerned, which will provide some space for the position of managers from that country to have some effect on the calculation. For example, in his discussion of Sweden, Ingham (1974, p. 27) notes that 'a native management in a company controlled by foreign capital may conceal labour "troubles" through fear of outside encroachments on their prerogative'. Equally, the decision to run down a particular plant's operations will normally involve a management strategy in that country over a considerable time period which again will normally make space for the local management to have an input into the decision. Such points are commonplaces of the management literature – see for example Brooke and van Beusekom (1979, p. 140), 'Some enterprises claim to plan entirely from the top downwards. Usually this turns out to be an aspiration rather than the reality.'

Multinationals then are constrained, like all organizations, by the inescapable if variable exigencies of their organizational pattern. But there is alongside this the question of what strategy a multinational would pursue, allowing for this purpose that this strategy was readily realizable. At the moment most multinational companies do *not* have a 'global strategy'. 'In general it is the U.S. firms which have advanced most rapidly in the development of global strategies, although even amongst U.S. firms it is still the minority which is endeavouring to operate fully integrated strategies. Most European multinationals are much less co-ordinated' (Channon and Jalland 1979, p. 10). Clearly this position is important because a lot of the fears about multinationals seem to assume that they operate global strategies within which switching capacity around the globe is a readily available option. There may be tendencies towards such a strategy but for many companies they are not yet realized (Vernon 1977, Ch. 2). In addition it may be noted that the development towards such strategies is ambiguous in its effects on the bargaining power of multinationals

118

in relation to national governments. For if the global strategy takes the form of an integrated series of plants, different components of a final product being produced in different countries, the bargaining power of the national government may be increased compared with where for example each country produces its own quota of the final product. In the former case the disruption to the overall position of the company by withdrawing from one country would seem to be much greater, and therefore the capacity of the government (or trade unions) to determine the conditions of operating in such a country correspondingly greater.

V

The argument of this chapter has not at all been that socialists have nothing to worry about in the growth of large firms and multi-nationals. The first issue is whether the growth of such entities can be considered so fundamental to the economy as to justify the centrality they are given in discussion of the economy by many socialists, and to justify talking of them as meaning a wholly new stage to capitalism. The argument of this chapter is obviously that these changes do not have anything like this signficance. Whilst the growth of the scale of the typical business enterprise and the growth in the role of multinationals raise many important problems for socialists, these problems are different in degree rather than in kind from the problems that private business corporations have always posed for socialist politics.

Secondly whilst accepting that large firms and multinationals are major loci of economic decision-making in the capitalist economy, the approach which has dominated socialist (and much other) discussion of these firms has been that around the monopoly/competition dichotomy. In this chapter it has been argued that this approach to large firms is at best dubious, depending on theoretical vagueness and often claiming much more than can be plausibly demonstrated. If on the contrary the focus is on these firms precisely as sites of decision-making which, because of their scale, have widespread effects, then the way is open firstly to examine the complexity of these decision-making practices, an examination which cannot to any substantial degree be aided by a simple monopoly/competition dichotomy. Secondly to analyse in what ways this decision-making can be subject to scrutiny, regulation and accountability (a problem returned to in the next chapter). To put the point slightly differently: whilst I have

119

argued that much of the Labour Left's position *does* exaggerate both the importance and capacities of large capitalist enterprises, sometimes in almost demonic ways, the problem is also that the way in which these enterprises are approached by the Left is an inadequate one, an approach unable to cope with the very substantial role that these enterprises *do* play.

A central point in the discussion of mesoeconomic companies was that typically socialists work with an inadequately developed notion of competition. Concerned to attack those who would see in competition the solution to all economic problems, but wanting to stress the noncompetitive nature of capitalist industry, they conflate a variety of different effects of competition in a way which unhelpfully locks the argument into 'for or against' competition. Competition can perhaps helpfully be seen as one means amongst many by which firms' activities are determined, neither its presence or absence having an absolutely determinant effect on that activity. Competition (and correlatively the terms on which economic agents participate in markets) can then be conceived as *one* object of policy which might be pursued by socialists in relation to some enterprises, rather than as a mechanism which is in principle anathema to socialists. The question then becomes how far, under what conditions, in which sectors of the economy might competition achieve certain specified ends (low price, good product quality, etc.), how could these conditions be achieved, and how could they be made compatible with other socialist objectives *vis-à-vis* the enterprise rather than how can competition be suppressed.

In relation to multinationals a similar point can be made: multinationality of itself implies no necessary strategy or structure in the enterprise and it is in relation to these strategies and structures that policies need to be evolved. In particular this involves taking seriously the organizational constraints on these companies as well as the organizational constraints of governments. An evaluation of multinationals which argues that 'This new form of organisation, based upon a flexible internal structure and on the capacity to mobilize vast resources towards the development of new technology, can effectively integrate and orchestrate world-wide operations, thus acquiring a monopolistic control over key sectors of production' (Faundez and Piciotto 1978, p. 1) greatly understates these constraints and in doing so exaggerates the impact of multinationals on the political possibilities for socialist regulation of such enterprises.

120

Whilst socialists have tended to homogenize the multinationals, the prospects for socialist action must be partly based on understanding and playing on the *differences* between such enterprises. Thus for example whilst decisions over major financial flows may normally be made at a central headquarters, these as already suggested are to a greater or lesser extent dependent on information from the management at lower levels of the organization. In other areas of company strategy – industrial relations, work organization, marketing – policy may well be formally more decentralized. And strategies may differ *within* any one enterprise depending on the nature of the product – most multinationals being also multi-product.

[margin note: required skill labour dependent on natural resources i.e. nickel.]

In its evaluation of monopoly and multinationals, socialist argument still remains remarkably orthodox① despite its heterodox rhetoric. At one level it is commonly orthodox Keynesianism, where that implies an exaggeration of the capacity of governments in capitalist countries to achieve their objectives; the other side of this is an underestimation of the constraints on any government policy, including a socialist government. At another level this Keynesian orthodoxy is undercut by the importation of conceptions of competition, monopoly, free flow of capital, etc. from neo-classical economics which are used as a way of offsetting the macroeconomic bias of Keynesianism, but in a form which seems to raise more problems than it solves. Of course socialist studies of firms' organizations and practices are vital and urgent, but socialists will probably learn much more on this from management, accounting and organizational literature than they will from neo-classical microeconomics. With all its great variety, this latter seems to suffer from an irreducible problem of conceiving economic agents as rational calculators always (in principle) capable of attaining their objective. Some parts at least of these 'practical' disciplines escape this disabling problem.

This last point links to a central characteristic of Holland and many other similar socialist arguments. At stake in much of such discussions of the capitalist enterprise is the notion of *power* – mesoeconomic/multinational firms get power from national governments whose power is in consequence reduced. Recent arguments (e.g. Minson 1980) as to the vacuity of the concept of power are therefore relevant to the current argument, but as they are also relevant to other parts of this book this point will be taken up at some length in Chapter 7.

① – conventional.

NOTE

1 Though the relationship may well not be a linear one, but dependent upon a crucial threshold level, above and below this level the profit-ability/concentration relationship is a statistically poor one (see Dalton and Penn 1976). For a general survey of the literature see Cowling *et al.* (1980, Ch. 12).

CHAPTER SEVEN

Socialist objectives
and
capitalist enterprises

The framework of this chapter is as follows. The starting point is the problem of conceptualizing capitalist enterprises and the (in part) consequential problems of discussing socialist objectives in relation to such enterprises. Both of these problems are examined in relation to existing socialist positions, drawing upon and going beyond the discussion of these in the preceding chapters. This also involves stressing the way in which socialist positions on the enterprise are commonly implicated in extremely dubious general theories of social relations.

The conceptualization of the enterprise which has already been hinted at (e.g. Chapter 3) is one which is a partial analogue to Donzelot's conception of the family (Donzelot 1980; see also Hodges and Hussain 1979; Hirst 1981a). In Donzelot families are treated as the points of intersection of a variety of practices (medical, judicial, educational, psychiatric, etc.) which define the family in a variety of ways, as a unit of habitation, as a child-rearing unit, as a unit of marital relations, as a locus of domestic tasks, as a financial unit, etc. This cuts across notions of the family as having any essential function or any clear-cut boundaries. Donzelot uses this conception of the family to contest the major discourses on the family – feminist, Marxist, psychoanalytic – which all in different ways construct the family as having some essential function (feminism the subordination of women, Marxism the reproduction of labour power and the ruling ideology, psychoanalysis perhaps an unstable mixture of the two).

Now the contention here is that a similar conception of the enterprise can produce a similarly productive disruption of some existing discussions of capitalist enterprises.

What may seem a rather perverse starting point in analysing enterprises has two major fruitful consequences. Firstly it cuts across any definition which conceives of capitalist enterprises as having any essential function subordinating all others. This does not itself challenge the adequacy of any one particular mode of conceptualizing the enterprise – as a labour process for example – which is a separate question, but challenges the way in which *any* such function is elevated to a determining role.

Secondly and correlatively such an approach brings into focus the importance of the diverse boundaries which can be drawn around the enterprise and thereby 'de-centres' any form of intervention which might be posed as a socialist objective *vis-à-vis* such enterprises. Thus socialist objectives must recognize both the absence of a simple hierarchy of determination between different practices within the enterprise, and that for different objectives different boundaries need to be drawn in talking of the enterprise. Both these points will be returned to and illustrated below.

It is important to say what this 'Donzelotian' notion of the enterprise *does not* imply. Firstly it does not imply that all an enterprise's practices should be treated as on a par, but that focusing on any particular one can only be a consequence of a political calculation as to the objectives to be given priority rather than as a consequence of the 'reality' of the enterprise. For example for some socialist concerns (the composition of output, the level of employment for example) the enterprise as a unit constrained to reproduce itself financially whilst engaging in commodity exchange (Bettelheim 1976, Pt 2, Ch. 2) can be argued to be central.

But it is important to stress that this is *not* to reproduce the notion of capitalist enterprises as fundamentally profit-maximizing entities in a slightly different guise. Firstly because the notion of 'financially reproducing' rather than 'profit-maximizing' is used to bring out the looseness of such a constraint. Where profit-maximizing is often taken to imply an end to which only one set of means are adequate, financial reproduction can be seen as guaranteed by extremely diverse means. For example, as the recession of the early 1980s has amply demonstrated, tardy payment of debts and pressure on debtors keep many a company going (and inability to do this dooms many a small business to bankruptcy). Equally, government grants, tax allowances and subsidies seem in many cases to be a crucial component of company cash flow.

Secondly financial reproduction is different from many notions of profit maximization in that it does not imply the subordination of the enterprise practices to a 'goal'. (And the same point would apply to other posited goals, e.g. satisficing). Alternatively one can say that the way profit criteria operate within companies varies enormously. In some cases every detailed operation is calculated in relation to profit calculations, in others profit is as it appears in the balance sheet, a residual left over when all other payments have been made.

Thirdly, and this is a point returned to below, capitalist enterprises can be defined for many purposes wholly independently of any *legal* status.

By the same token, to return to the general point, the 'Donzelotian' notion of the enterprise does not deny that the various practices of enterprises are the object of co-ordination by agents within the enterprise and that to a degree this co-ordination is successful. But by initially focusing on the aspects of diversity rather than co-ordination such a definition challenges a number of positions common within British socialism.

Commonly British socialism treats the enterprise as a locus of power of two kinds: as having power *vis-à-vis* other aspects of social relations – the economy 'in general' politics etc. – a power expressed in relation to agents 'external' to the enterprise (Holland (1976) is the obvious example). This point will be returned to. Relevant here however is the second notion of the enterprise as a locus of power, as a power 'structure' in which *within* the enterprise certain groups of agents are subject to the powers of others.

The notion of power here is similar to and equally problematic as the notion used in sociological and political theory. It involves notions of subjects who 'possess' power and use this power to dominate others – normally in socialist conceptions capitalist management has power and uses it to dominate workers.

Now we should be clear on what is objectionable in analysing enterprises in this way. Power used in this sense must be *unconditional* – the possession of power gives the capacity to dominate others. If the power were conditional then it could not be possessed in this way and so collapses as a coherent notion. It would cease to have a determinate locus and the outcome of any determinate struggle would become dependent not upon a prior distribution of power but upon the particular forces and relations between forces deployed in the particular arena of struggle (Minson 1980, p. 24).

Power or its analogue in this context 'control' can thus never be the object of a simple displacement in its possession – from managers to workers for example. This *does not* mean that to talk of 'workers' control' is to talk in absurdities. 'Control', however, like the 'democracy' of the parallel slogan 'industrial democracy', must be seen as having meaning only in relation to specific sites of decision-making with specific constituencies exercising decision-making. 'Controlling' the enterprise must involve locating various points of decision-making in it and attempting to obtain effective control at these various points (points which will be arrayed in a contingent hierarchy).

This position would not in the first instance mark any clear distinction from the traditional socialist focus of claims for industrial democracy on company boards of directors. But it would imply that the effects of workers' control exercised by, say, a majority of worker representatives on a board of directors would not have sovereign powers over the enterprise. The decision-making capacity of such boards is and would remain necessarily constrained by the dispersion of decision-making within the enterprise which would be open to reconstruction (different definitions of competences, different divisions of labour, etc.) but could never be eliminated. Thus the almost totalitarian imagery of the enterprise conjured up by Holland *et al.* is inappropriate not only to the existing capitalist enterprise but to *any* enterprise – the exercise of workers' control could not eliminate this. (This is a different point from the clear attempts to reconstruct decision-making to evade 'industrial democracy' in recent experiments in Britain (see e.g. Worker Directors 1977).)

The idea that company boards do not exercise sovereign power is recognised *in a particular way* by many socialist arguments. This recognition is commonly based on the notion, discussed in Chapter 2, that the individual capitalist enterprise cannot escape its tight insertion into a wider set of social relations, this insertion being guaranteed by two mechanisms, profit-seeking and/or interest representation. The capitalist enterprise is forced to function in certain ways because profit-making entails a single set of deducible consequences, or because within the enterprise there exist representatives of society-wide interests which effectively subordinate the enterprises' operations. Thus Hyman (1974, p. 252) chides the Institute for Workers' Control for its alleged excessive emphasis on individual industries, arguing that it is impossible to have 'socialism in one industry' because of 'virtually irresistible pressures to accommodate "realistically" to the coercive demands of market forces or government requirements'. Both these mechanisms of 'coercion' of the enterprise have already been touched on but they require further elaboration particularly because of the use made of them by socialists such as Hyman.

In Chapter 2 the role of decision-making in the enterprise was linked to military strategy, where strategy was used to suggest a 'field' of decision-making rather than the concept of a simple line of deduction from profit-seeking to enterprise practices. But simple notions of military strategy can imply precisely the kind of totalitarian entity being argued against here. Once a general makes a decision it is simply passed down the line until every soldier has carried out the order from on high. This of course is *not* an adequate account of military strategy (see e.g. Keegan 1976).

Strategy is commonly used in something close to this sense in discussions of the enterprise. In Chandler's (1962) famous study, for example, strategy is defined (p. 13) as the 'determination of the basic long-term goals and objectives of an enterprise, and the adoption of courses of action and the allocation of resources necessary for carrying out these goals'. This is of course the very standard rationalist argument where a subject (human or non-human) has intentions which it attempts successfully or unsuccessfully to realize (Hindess 1977, 1978). Now it may be the case that it is difficult to discuss the enterprise and avoid such formulations altogether, in the same way as rationalism is equally problematic and equally difficult to avoid in politics in general. But at a minimum the problems of such a position need to be brought out. In the current context the problem is above all that such rationalistic formulations greatly overstate the subordination of the practices of the enterprise in a hierarchy where the goal (*whatever* it might be) sits at the apex. This is not simply to assert the role of 'tactical' flexibility within a strategic consensus, precisely because this takes for granted the 'overall' subordination of practices one to another.

Perhaps the term management rather than strategy should be used where management has the same sense as in the phrase 'management of the personality', that is management implies not so much control of other agents and their subordination to the achievement of a goal, but rather the containment of separate and often contradictory practices[1] – a matter of 'keeping the show on the road'. Management is then seen as facing such problems as 'how can the practices of sub-agency A be made compatible with those of B?' and 'how can the decisions of C be minimized in their negative impact on D?' rather than how the practices of A, B, C, D can be subordinated to the goals of the enterprise.

This is not to deny that much management literature does present the enterprise as a subject endowed with goals and the management problem as how to achieve them most effectively. And this approach, through being embodied in management literature, has its effects. Indeed, in the sense that enterprises do succeed in producing outputs, some degree of 'goal-achievement' is attained. But the important point is that this conception of strategy is consonant with the notions of the 'sovereign' board of directors, which, with that of other sovereign loci of power, needs to be contested.

The stress on enterprise strategy as a holding together, a perpetual re-coupling of diverse practices within the enterprise, also conflicts with the notions of strategy employed in many socialist accounts of the enterprise.

Braverman (1974) has been particularly influential in Britain. His work is on the dividing line between a conception of the enterprise which sees its practices as simply deduced from profit objectives and one which sees it as having a guiding strategy. From a postulation of profit maximization is deduced a single managerial strategy – securing managerial control over the labour process by separating manual and mental labour and consequently de-skilling the work-force. Leaving aside any general assessment of Braverman's work (see Cutler 1978), what is clear is that in this version the enterprise is very much seen as having a goal with unambiguous consequences which are in general realised. So we have a 'radical' version of Chandler – the goals differ (in Chandler labour rather than being central is simply one 'resource' to be used) but the conception of the enterprise is markedly similar.

Now it has become a commonplace of the recent Marxist literature on Braverman to contest his unilateralism, stressing either the importance of opposition ('the class struggle'), which inhibits the realization of management goals (e.g. Elger 1979), or arguing that the goal of the capitalist enterprise can be achieved by *different* strategies

(Friedman 1977). What neither contest is the subordination in principle of the enterprise to an unambiguous goal. Different roads exist, but different roads to the same place. The road may be blocked, but the capitalist will continue to try to get through.

The point to be stressed here is not that the capitalist enterprise will not have a financial strategy, nor that it will have an 'industrial relations' strategy. The point is the relation between these strategies. In most socialist accounts the relation is one of super/subordination where the financial strategy (profit maximization) leads to the industrial relations strategy ('control' of the workforce by de-skilling, etc.). This cannot register the problematic status of one strategy with respect to the other; for example even within Braverman's framework it is far from clear that de-skilling is functional for profit-making given the inherent creativity and intransigence of human labour. But more important, what is the basis for the assumption that those carrying out the industrial relations strategy are effectively subordinated to those pursuing a financial strategy? For example a particular industrial relations strategy may be presented and accepted by the body corporate as the only viable one, and the financial strategy tailored to reflect it. Or perhaps the relation between financial and industrial relations strategy will remain always a contested one, neither subordinate to the other.

This point can be extended in two directions. An industrial relations strategy will itself involve a holding together of a range of practices, recruitment, supervision, payments systems, safety – various areas of negotiation which are both diverse in themselves and not hermetically sealed from other strategies. Obviously, for example, wages are the object of calculation on the part of both financial managers and managers of industrial relations. Secondly the sets of practices to be co-ordinated are not just financial and industrial relations but also production itself, distribution, sales, advertising, etc.

The diversity of practices within enterprises also poses problems for the other pole of the insertion of capitalist enterprises into 'wider' social relations, that of interest representation. The simple conception of a global strategy of profit maximization common in socialist discussion of the enterprises conceives the enterprises as the particular site of a general struggle between two interests – capitalists versus workers. The strategy of the enterprise management is then the representation of one of those interests (capitalists) in its objective of combating the interests of the others (workers). So here, in the analysis of the enterprise, it should be stressed that the concepts of interests and their representation are active as they are in so many other parts of socialist ideology.

The objections to conceiving enterprises in this way needs spelling out with some care. The objection cannot be to talking of interests at all – this seems unavoidable in any discussion of social relations. The question is *how* they are to be talked about. In many discussions, not only those by the Left, interests are seen as pre-given by social relations in general, outside any particular arena. Thus when socialists talk about the interests of the working class these interests are seen as derived from the place of the working class in capitalism and as existing in principle entirely separate of any means of calculating them. These interests exist in and through particular forms of representation (e.g. in the enterprise) but they are not affected by these forms, the interest remains the same whatever the form. Thus the interests of a female part-time cleaner in a university are the same as those of a full-time male air traffic controller at Heathrow. Of course such examples as these have 'short-term' interests in addition but fundamentally the shared status of workers overrides any such 'short-term' particularities. Not only are the fundamental interests of workers derivative of social relations in general but also any attachment of interest to agencies other than that of 'the class'[2] must be seen as an error – a misunderstanding of capitalist realities. This conception of interest has been used by socialists on occasion to attack measures taken by a particular group of workers to aid the survival of the enterprise they work in because this is seen as detracting from the pursuit of the interests of *all* workers (e.g. Coventry 1980, p. 108).[3] In this way the postulation of a general interest must act to hamstring any struggle which falls short of realizing that general interest (i.e. socialism).

In practice this problem is of course avoided by means of a variety of *ad hoc* strategies by socialists but it needs stressing as a theoretical problem. It is no good arguing that there is no such general interest (for example socialism is against the interests of the working class) but the negative impact of such a conception on talking about, *inter alia*, the enterprise should be stressed. Once discarded there is no clear reason why for example workers' control of capitalist firms (in the sense of financially reproducing commodity exchangers) should be seen as problematic *in principle* for socialists. The notion of workers and their representatives being detrimentally 'incorporated' goes by the board if there is no theory of general interests to be incorporated into. Equally the objection to inter-worker, via inter-enterprise, competition on grounds of its cutting across the general interest also falls (though it may be objectionable on other grounds).

One can say therefore that in terms of formulating positive socialist policies the notion of socialist *objectives* rather than interests should be used. Socialist politics is then not the articulation of and support for pre-existing interests but the formulation of objectives and the construction of constituencies of support for such objectives. Arguments that such objectives are in the interests of political constituencies may be one mode of mobilizing support for these objectives, but only one. Interests may in this framework be commonly seen as constraints on objectives because of their attachment to existing forms of organization, and therefore as obstructions to generating constituencies behind proposals to reform those organizations.

Side-stepping these pre-given interests also cuts across much of the socialist discussion of trade unionism in relation to claims for industrial democracy (as well as trade unionism in other contexts). The common measuring rod for such claims is the extent to which workers in industrial democracy structures (for example representation on the board of directors) are 'truly' represented (see Chapter 2). Thus for example in Hyman (1974) one gets a coupling of an essence of trade unionism with a conception that because this essence under capitalism is *at best* only partially socialist (it is not truly representative of workers' interests) 'single channel' representation via trade unions will always be inadequate. This leads to opposition to a single channel of representation because this 'subordinates potential agencies of self-management to the existing priorities of collective bargaining' (p. 250). The point is not of course that existing trade unions are ideal institutions of industrial democracy but is rather the unhelpfulness of looking at this issue in terms of essentialized forms of representation of pre-given interests.

The general notion of representation deployed in socialist arguments is also relevant to the enterprise – trade unions or any other means of representation must unavoidably partly construct what is represented (Hirst 1978). This is *not* an argument for autonomy of union representatives from their constituents, but a recognition that their position, like that of any other representatives, cannot be one of mouthpiece. Accountability, recallability are clearly desirable but they have unbreakable limits.

Once it is accepted that the enterprise has a diversity of functions and around each interests will be constructed, then clearly socialist objectives must not only take account of this diversity but must also accept that different socialist objectives may not be compatible in the enterprise. Again this point is recognized *in a particular way* by socialists, a common concern being how can some form of centralized planning of the economy be made compatible with workers' control of the enterprise. In some cases the problem is spirited away by invoking 'democratic planning' but whatever its uses as a slogan this is clearly more a problem than an adequate solution (Fox 1978, p. 17). But leaving aside such 'solutions' the problem with this formulation is that it is predicated upon a dichotomy of particular versus general interest rather than a specification of *objectives* to be pursued. If this latter is done, then at one level the problem is worsened because there are many more than two interests which may attach themselves to the practices that socialists want to change. But also in a sense the problem is eased because of the recognition that the socialist objective can never be the once-and-for-all resolution of conflicts of interests but must rather be an attempt to adjust such conflicts and co-ordinate them in a particular fashion.

I

What then is the diversity of objectives that socialists may pursue in relation to capitalist enterprise?

Democracy

In this respect enterprises are no different from any unit of organization. The precise meaning of democracy is always ambiguous but is taken here to mean major decision-making positions being elective and where the constituency for such elections is determined by those working within the enterprise. Such electoral processes obviously have the same kind of conditions of existence as such processes have elsewhere – availability of information on candidates, access to means of distribution of election material, etc. But there are two important and specific conditions which are important for socialist accounts of the enterprise.

The first is size. As argued when discussing G.D.H. Cole, it is important to stress the links between effective democracy and size, smallness of size facilitating the spread of the knowledge and competence necessary for such democracy. Here the question of divergent boundaries of enterprises is central. 'Size' here can apply to any unit subject to a degree of unity of command such that important decision-making capacities exist at the level of command in relation to that unit. These units may well not coincide with units determined by other criteria, for example they may not be financially self-producing, they may not be coterminous with the legal boundaries of enterprises. This would be true of the typical multi-plant large firm in Britain where each plant is a unit of command but may not be a financial unit, and also commonly true within particular production processes within a plant. A strategy for industrial democracy would have to seek to multiply such units of command staying within large-scale companies in the legal and financial sense predominantly, but also wherever possible press for companies where units of command coincide with legal and financial units, i.e. small firms and co-operatives. The latter would be especially significant in non-manufacturing where legally small units are predominant.

Much of the existing structure of British industry owes little to any rational criterion, but is the accidental by-product of financial speculation, government-encouraged merger or the unintended by-product of corporate acquisitions. Thus, to propose as central a reconstruction of the organization of industry to facilitate democracy is not to propose a 'utopian' strategy against a brutally rational existing system. There is great scope for reorganization, for instance by splitting off marketing, research, design and other 'peripheral' functions from manufacturing activities and handing them over to democratic small firms and co-operatives.

However it must be accepted that even in the event of such radical reorganization the form of democracy will be different as between large firms with elaborate managerial hierarchies (hierarchies may be altered but cannot simply be dissolved) and small-scale co-operatives. Recognizing the diversity of the practices of enterprises means recognizing the diversity of forms of worker democracy also. Thus 'direct' forms of democracy may be possible either in small co-operatives or in relation to, say, immediate work practices in a large enterprise; less direct forms of democracy must often be adopted in relation to broad corporate strategies.

Such a strategy of democratization would have no unambiguous relation to other objectives – it *might* be functional to some notions of efficiency (especially in Britain with its often grotesque managerial practices), but the important point to make is that there is no single scale along which its effects might be measured. It needs therefore to be argued for in its own right. 'In its own right' means that democracy is a preferred form of social organization for socialists. This raises a number of problems. First 'democracy' is one of those words bandied about in political argument with little discussion of its meaning. Here 'democracy' means simply that personnel for certain posts be subject to election rather than some other mode of appointment, and this in turn means that certain other conditions – freedom of circulation of election propaganda, non-prohibitive qualifications to stand, multiplicity of candidates – must be fulfilled to make the election more than a token exercise.

Democracy is therefore a specific political mechanism and *not* the realization of an individual 'right' (Hirst 1981a, p. 62). What is represented on elected bodies will depend on the precise nature of the mechanisms of the election – the constituency, the manner in which votes are aggregated, etc. Thus it is impossible to conceive of electoral mechanisms which do not have of themselves political consequences dependent upon the type of these mechanisms. In the case of the Bullock proposals for example the mechanisms proposed were clearly designed to represent the objectives of the trade unions and shop stewards at the level of company policy.

Even if it is argued that company board elections should *not* be based on trade unions in the way suggested by Bullock, it has to be recognized that any alternative would be equally 'biased' in its effects. For example any company-based elections would seem likely to require some qualifying period before the voter becomes part of the electorate, perhaps combined with a minimum number of hours worked. This would clearly 'bias' the electoral process, depending on the composition and turnover of the labour force. The point to be emphasized is that even if Bullock had argued for 'universal suffrage' in board elections, this would no more create a 'true representation' than a narrower electorate. (How much difference the latter would in fact have made seems debatable given the high level of trade union organization in the size of companies relevant to the Bullock proposals.)

The central points in discussion of industrial democracy would then seem to boil down to these. Firstly socialists should be in favour of democratic procedures, in the sense outlined above, as a matter of political principle. (Whilst recognizing that this argument may have its limits – in some areas (brain surgeons?) questions of competence may override the democratic preference, though in fact the choice will rarely be black and white.) Secondly they need to recognize that this principle will always involve definite electoral mechanisms which will always have their own effects. The means of representation will always in part construct what is represented. Thirdly, bearing in mind the second point, proposals for 'democratization' have to be coupled with specific political objectives to be fought for in democratic arenas. Or to put the point slightly differently, democracy cannot be seen as of itself functional to socialist objectives. In the case of industrial democracy it may cause as many problems for such objectives (e.g. inter-enterprise equality) as it solves.

Such a strategy would link to the other major component of effective democracy – changes in the division of labour. In social democratic advocacies of industrial democracies (e.g. Bray and Falk 1974; Fabians 1976; Oakeshott 1978) such democracy is coupled to a continuation of existing divisions of labour; the roles of agents remain the same and only the relationship between them alters, that is workers elect managers. But industrial democracy, by focusing on the competence of the agents, by being linked to particular decision-making procedures, opens up questions concerning the way in which the tasks allocated to the elected are so allocated. Equally, because effective democratic control depends on the *dispersion* of competences, the existing division of labour based on non-dispersion is thrown into the melting pot. (We leave aside here the radical implications for patterns of education and training of any such re-division of labour.)

Because of the pertinence to its achievement of size and the division of labour, industrial democracy is potentially much more radical in its implications than the consensual advocacy of it by the Centre-Left implies. But equally industrial democracy cannot helpfully be conceived of as the realization of an interest where that interest is conceived as an end to which democracy is the means. Its consequences are too incalculable for that.

Regulation[4]

Regulation is commonly seen as the intervention of the 'public sphere' into the 'private domain' of the enterprise and in part socialist discussions are concerned with the proper scope of such intervention. Here again Donzelot's analysis of the family is instructive by demonstrating the impossibility of sustaining a consistent separation of private and public, showing how the practices of agents within the family are inescapably conditioned by factors external to it. The same point can be made in relation to enterprises – there may be practices within enterprises which are not the object of regulation but this does not create a separate sphere of private activity separate from the public domain.

Equally the link between the practices of enterprises with respect to aspects of social relations cannot helpfully be seen in the form of enterprise 'power' over these other aspects. This is not to dispute the scale of the resources available to many modern enterprises nor the wide ramifications of their activities. But as with the notion of 'power' internal to the enterprise, powers exercised externally cannot be seen as deriving from a sovereign source and bound together by an all-embracing strategy which subordinates everything to its all-seeing gaze.

One obvious implication of this is that any measure couched in terms of the capture of this sovereign power *must* be inadequate. This role is of course usually played in socialist arguments by nationaliz-ation. The subject of nationalization will be returned to later, but the implication of posing 'regulation' as the objective as opposed to nationalization is precisely to register the multi-faceted nature of the enterprise and the multiplicity of socialist goals with respect to it.

One major form of regulation of the enterprise is the market. This is not, however, the way in which the market is commonly conceived by socialists, especially perhaps in Britain. For example a representative sample of socialist writing on the economy such as Green and Nore (1977) provides practically no discussion of markets except in a criticism of 'consumer sovereignty' which implies that market regulation of enterprise is somehow unimportant because the 'pur-pose' of production is accumulation (see also Aaronovitch and Smith 1981, p. 250).

There seem to be two major reasons for the rejection of the market as a mode of regulation of enterprises by socialists. First the magic formula of classical and neo-classical economics, where the individual pursuit of self-interest is said to bring about the maximum welfare of all, is turned on its head and only those practices which are seen as 'consciously controlled' are seen as being functional to the general welfare, the welfare of the working class if not of society as a whole. This then leads to a plan/market dichotomy where the 'conscious control' is opposed to the anarchy of the market. Once again we can see how the intervention of vaguely formulated and unquestioned general concepts of social relations – in this case the conscious individual as subject of philosophical humanism – intrudes into socialist arguments on the enterprise.

In addition to this plan/market dichotomy there is a focus on commodities as *signs* of the existence of certain forms of social relations. The existence of commodities is treated as evidence of the nature of the economic system as a whole – its essence rather than as consequences of the status and relations between particular economic agents. Classically this was the case in the example of the New Economic Policy in the Soviet Union in the 1920s. Here the re-introduction of legalized commodity relations was generally registered as a partial defeat on the road to total victory for socialism, conceived as the suppression of these relations. This is clearly opposed to those notions which see commodity relations as having effects only in relation to their specific participants (Littlejohn 1979).

Despite the attacks on the plan/market dichotomy and its correlation, the treatment of commodities as signs (e.g. Brus 1972; Bettelheim 1976; Bettelheim and Sweezy 1971), the suppression of market relations is still commonly treated by British socialism as its ultimate objective. For example in Coventry (1980) there is a simple opposition 'market' versus 'social needs' (e.g. p. 78) which reproduces precisely these notions.

There is one other aspect to this general blindness which is worthy of note. Much effort by the Left in Britain goes into denying the 'legitimacy' of private industry provided by the proponents of consumer sovereignty (Holland 1976). The task is seen as one of exposing the fraudulence of these claims to legitimacy which then becomes *de facto* a case for socialism. Thus if it can be shown that the market doesn't really respond to human wants and needs, this exposes the lie at the heart of capitalism's case. This leads to a confrontation between the proponents of markets and consumer sovereignty, like the Institute of Economic Affairs, and those who argue, like Holland (1978, p. 156): 'Under conditions of monopoly domination of the main markets in the economy producer power is sovereign, subject to the dictates and criteria of capital, and largely imposing decisions on what should be produced, why, where, how, when and for whom on both labour and the consumer.'

Against this it can simply be argued that markets have determinate and differential consequences on the agents who participate, including enterprises, and these may be fully compatible with *some* socialist objectives. Firstly as far as consumer durable goods go markets are commonly a very effective means of satisfying consumer wants. Socialists commonly obscure this point by pointing to the alleged impact of advertising in shaping these wants. But advertising as an explanation of patterns of consumption is being asked to bear too much weight here. In the same way that, as Donzelot argues, 'ideology' cannot explain the generality of attachment to family relationships, advertising cannot explain our attachment to motor cars, hi-fis and household gadgets. Consumers are not blank sheets of paper upon which anything can be written. There often seems to lurk behind socialists attacks on advertising a puritan distaste of consumption *per se* to which Crosland in particular rightly objected (and clearly demonstrated his personal exemption from).

Of course markets have severe limitations as a means of satisfying consumer wants, as neo-classical welfare economics has for long and lovingly detailed. For a recent excellent example see Hirsch (1977). But for many classes of goods it cannot easily be improved upon, indeed it may be *preferable* to the non-market forms – queueing, patronage, etc. – so extensively experimented with in Eastern Europe.

It is more or less the same with the notion of efficiency. Here the position is not so much that socialists have objected to the means of attaining the objective, but that they have been unhappy with conceding it as an objective at all (an exception to this is mentioned below in the discussion of nationalization). Now suspicion of efficiency criteria is justified in part because of the profound ambiguity of the term (Hall and Winsten 1959), but it can be defined in such a way as to have an important role to play in socialist objectives. In the UK, with its high level of imports of foodstuffs and raw materials, a measure of success in international competition is vital for maintaining let alone improving the standard of living. This means that in almost any conceivable circumstance Britain will have to be a successful competitor in international trade, which must be in large measure a consequence of enterprise 'efficiency', that is to say the provision of goods of high enough quality and low enough price to secure a ready sale abroad. To reject such competitive success is of course possible but its consequences for the standard of living, and therefore *one* condition of socialist support, must be substantial. To do so would impose enormous political costs with no clear offsetting benefits.

Focusing on efficiency in this sense is commonly opposed by socialists because (a) it defines efficiency in relation to markets and not social needs (e.g. Coventry 1980, p. 78), and (b) it is commonly assumed to be achievable only in one way. 'There is little doubt that if the goal of restructuring is to be a competitive success, then some such onslaught on working class living standards and power is necessary' (ibid.). On the contrary, efficiency, we may argue, is like profits, there is no royal road to its achievement, only a set of strategies which may treat it as a differentially calculated objective.

Once efficiency is treated as an objective it seems clear that competition in the market place is *one* means to its achievement. Clearly it has to be augmented, above all because the market does not *dictate* efficient practices to enterprises, in the way much British industrial policy discussion implies, let alone provide the conditions and know-how for their implementation. Rather it provides nothing more than a measure of the success or failure of various enterprise strategies. The appropriate response to 'failure' in the market cannot be deduced from the failure itself.

Here there would seem to be an important role for what might be called compulsory management consultancy. This seems to have been the role played by the Price Commission under the 1974–9 Labour government, a regulation of efficiency within the enterprise imposed as a condition of scrutiny of requested price increases.[5] This is *not* the same as the also important proposals for 'social audit' of companies suggested long ago by Michael Barratt-Brown (1968b), those carried out by such organizations as Counter Information Services, and as proposed on a more general scale in *Labour's Programme 1973* (also Rowthorn and Ward 1980). These latter aim to displace current modes of accounting for enterprises by carrying out cost-benefit analyses which change the 'boundaries' of the calculation and so change the assessment of company policies. The former point is a narrower one, to bring to bear on all enterprises particular competences concerning managerial organization, work practices, etc. which will have a pay-off in the market place. This of course implies that there *are* managerial competences which must be in some manner deployed in any effective enterprise. This does not mean taking seriously every piece of nonsense promulgated as 'management science', but it does mean that certain definite managerial skills relating to such areas as production design, financial appraisal, etc. must be taken seriously and not reduced simply to obfuscatory emanations of an all-embracing capitalist interest. A socialist strategy would seem to need agencies of both these types.

One form of regulation which has been widely advocated by much of the British Left over the last decade or so is planning agreements, which form a central part of the AES (see CSE London Group 1980; Aaronovitch 1981). Planning agreements in this literature are seen as a good weapon but one which was not properly used under the Labour government of 1974–9. Whilst compulsory agreements of this kind clearly have a role to play, their centrality to a strategy of regulation of the private sector raises a number of problems.

One is that the planning agreements become too overloaded with objectives – they are charged with accomplishing every governmental ambition.[6] This is in principle dubious and relies on the notion of the firm as having the kind of 'totalitarian' structure already criticized, where each policy neatly meshes into every other and the whole is a neatly co-ordinated set.

Secondly the instrument of direct pressure on the firm is financial, the giving of government aid being tied to the conformity with government objectives. However whilst companies are likely to be affected by this, their dependence on governmental financial aid is not so overwhelming as to make compliance automatic. Financial sticks and carrots have been the staple diet of British industrial policy in the post-war period and have not proved an overwhelming success, and it is not clear how planning agreements would radically improve upon this.

Given the above points, planning agreements seem ill-adapted to the macroeconomic, especially investment-raising, objective to which the AES applies them. Indeed it can be argued that as advocated by proponents of this strategy they are likely to lead to a greater attachment of workers within an enterprise to enterprise-specific objectives. This in turn is likely to be a problem as much as a solution for economy-wide policy objectives (see on this Burchell and Tomlinson 1982).

The deficiencies of planning agreements derive not only from the particular problems noted above but also more generally from the idea of one kind of regulatory agency or institution being the mainstay of a regulatory strategy. This raises the problem of the kind of appropriate regulatory 'regime'.

First, as already implied, the need is for a *multiplicity* of regulatory agencies relating to different aspects of enterprise activity, none of them attempting to 'control' this activity but to bias it in a variety of policy-guided directions. Secondly it needs to be stressed that the institutions of regulation are themselves of importance. There already exists in the UK a variety of regulatory bodies – Equal Opportunities Commission, Commission for Racial Equality, Manpower Services Commission, for example, all of which to a greater or lesser extent impinge on enterprise practices. But each of these is characterizied by appointed executives, lack of accountability and arguably dominated by fairly narrow and administrative conceptions of their role. Clearly socialists who favour a regime of regulation would have to include as an objective the reform of such agencies in a democratic and accountable direction.

Thirdly these regulatory agencies would not themselves be sub-ordinated to any one overriding policy goal. For example there is obviously a case for devising a range of interventions seeking to raise the level of employment. But alongside this would be agencies concerned with for example questions of efficiency (in the sense defined above), the pursuit of which might well cut across employ-ment objectives. Thus a regulatory regime would *not* be central planning by another name, it would reflect and work upon the divergent practices of the enterprise, not attempting to impose a monolithic pattern but biasing enterprise activity in a variety of ways.

One form of regulation which is important in its scope (though indeterminate in its outcome) is regulation of accounting practices. The importance of accounting standards to corporate calculation and therefore activities has been well argued by G. Thompson (1978) and this is clearly an arena where up until now in the UK there has been an almost complete absence of socialist activity and proposals. The regulation of accounting practice has in consequence remained safely in the hands of the professional accounting bodies. Concern with accounting principles would link to the traditional Institute for Workers' Control stress on 'opening the books' (see Barratt-Brown 1968b), where this is seen as not simply an 'exposé' of the firm but signals an intent to comprehend in order to contest corporate strategies. Taken seriously such an objective requires a knowledge of accounting principles which in turn can be used to demonstrate their malleability, the fact that they are discursive forms with discursive and non-discursive consequences and conditions of existence and are not representations of an inescapable 'reality'.

Another important area of regulation is company law. A number of possibilities would seem open here. One would be a reform of company law which deprived shareholders of companies of their right to appoint directors which would leave them very much in a residual (though still important) position as simple creditors of the company. This would seem much preferable to the idea of promoting 'shareholder democracy' which has sometimes, oddly, gained favour on the Left (Labour Party 1974). This would seem a sensible correlate to any system of company-level industrial democracy.

Another possibility would be to see how far Swedish experiments with investment reserve funds could be adopted for use in the British context. These would seem a plausible weapon for a policy of promoting investment in employment-creating assets, though their success is obviously tied up with a whole range of other institutional features of Sweden, especially perhaps an 'active labour market' policy which it may be difficult to replicate in UK conditions (on the latter see Mukherjee 1972).

Plainly these points are extremely brief and general, but the central point at issue is the principle of mobilizing all kinds of different pressures and agencies which either already regulate enterprises or could relatively easily be constructed to do so. This of course would not be a means of simply defusing political opposition – a policy of effective investment reserve funds for example would be likely to arouse almost as much opposition as widespread nationalization. The point is that the former would more directly come to grips with some enterprise practices than the latter, would be more effective in gaining some socialist objectives.

New enterprises

Another objective that socialists might pursue is the creation of new enterprises; this would recognize the constraints on transforming enterprises producing one output into units of production of something else. Here again socialists have followed in their own idiosyncratic way the lines laid down by the broad consensus of industrial policy in Britain, which has been concerned with acting upon existing enterprises rather than encouraging the creation of new ones.

Of course starting new enterprises is an inherently risky undertaking. However good the modes of assessment of potentially successful new enterprises, failures are inevitable. But at the moment socialists are wholly ill-equipped to make any reasonable assessment of investment possibilities. Here again much is to be learned from existing management and perhaps especially management consultancy, not because these agents have large stocks of esoteric formal skills to deploy, but because they have (at best, see e.g. Boston 1975) the capacity to assess the variety of factors which enter into enterprise success and derive from this certain strategic guidelines. Such a capacity is surely required on the Left.[7]

II

Finally we return to the question of the role of nationalization. Clearly it follows from what has been said so far (and in Chapter 4) that nationalization cannot be the centrepiece of socialist objectives in relation to enterprises. This does not mean that nationalization has no role to play, only that it should be seen as one means amongst many.

Nationalization has been shown to be a powerful means to effect a rapid and massive shift of resources from one sector of an economy to another – especially from agriculture into industry. Equally it has been a powerful means to exploit new large-scale resources. In slightly different vein it could be a means to radically transform the lending practices of financial institutions.

Such objectives of nationalization mainly imply the 'old pattern' of British nationalization, which involves nationalization not of any particular enterprise but of a whole sector of the economy. Against this can be contrasted the recently popular arguments for nationalizing particular firms and allowing such publicly-owned firms to compete with the remaining private ones in that sector.

This was originally a 'revisionist' proposal from the Labour Right in the 1950s, and one at the time strongly objected to by most British socialists. The basis of these proposals in part derived from the focus by revisionism on equality as the central goal of socialism (Gaitskell 1956; Crosland 1956). 'Old-style' nationalization was argued to have had little impact on inequality in Britain. (Though, as Crosland himself noted (1956, Ch. xxii), 'old-style' nationalization had been based on a wide range of objectives, not simply that of equality.)

Crosland's advocacy of competitive public enterprise followed from

143

his general proposition that greater equality was only possible in the context of growth, and the object of these new public enterprises was to encourage such growth. Thus, he argued, firms should be nationalized in steel and machine tools to encourage expansion; where risks were too high for private producers, such as in atomic energy; where monopolies existed; and where industry required structural change (Crosland 1956, Ch. xxii). Such firms were to act as 'highly competitive price leaders and pace setters, provide a yardstick for efficiency, support the government's investment plans, and above all produce a better product of service' (Crosland 1974, p. 38).

Such an approach was clearly different from that traditional in British socialism where efficiency was not a major objective (it was largely conceived simply as a question of realizing *economies of scale* obstructed by private ownership, e.g. in the pits) and it rejected the stress on the role of the market place. The Gaitskell/Crosland version of nationalization is of course similar in some respects to that of Holland and the Labour Left of the 1970s. The differences lie not in the proposals but in their rationale. For Holland the objective of selective nationalization is to break the power of mesoeconomic firms (though complete nationalization remains the long-term goal – 1976, p. 179). The objectives are then multiple, paralleling the multiple obstruction placed in socialists' paths by mesoeconomic firms. This framework retains the notion of the sovereign firm, possessor of economic power. As a result, a heterogeneous range of socialist objectives are expected to be accomplished by the relatively simple expedient of confiscating that power.

The concept of nationalization cannot therefore be saved by its swathing in new clothes. It must be stressed again this does not mean that nationalization is wholly irrelevant to socialist objectives – nothing said above is intended to imply this. Rather the point to be stressed is the need to link proposals for nationalization to specific objectives and politically advantageous means of achieving such objectives, rather than coupling them to monolithic notions of power and sovereignty in and over the enterprise.

III

The introduction emphasized that this book, whilst focusing on the theories socialists have deployed in discussing capitalist enterprises, does not imply that all socialist political action can be reduced to the effects of these theories. Nevertheless the opposite supposition is surely equally fallacious; the signal failure of British socialism in relation to capitalist enterprises surely cannot be understood apart from the kinds of theories with which socialism has conceived its objectives. To put the point more strongly, any more successful politics must *in part* be predicated upon a rejection of much conceptual baggage with which the Left is encumbered.

The focus on enterprises in this book is not dependent upon any assumption that enterprises should in fact be the focal point of socialist politics. Rather this focus derives from the simple fact that enterprises have been and surely are likely to remain one important area of socialist political activity within almost any conceivable strategy.

More generally the arguments deployed above have, I hope, demonstrated how thin and weak socialist argument is in many crucial areas. In other words the 'conceptual baggage' of the Left has not only directly had adverse effects on the efficacy of its political activity, but has got in the way of other forms of *theoretical* activity which could provide one condition for more effective political activity. This is for example the case with 'the market'. For all its centrality in both defences and attacks upon capitalist social relations, this concept is remarkably underdeveloped. The heterogeneity of markets, even in the most sophisticated of 'mainstream' economics, is registered only by the rather simple notions of 'fix-price' and 'flex-price' as the two types of market form. And in more policy-oriented work even this distinction is lost in dichotomous market versus state formulae around which both anti and pro socialists are only too willing to take up their colours.

The above point is made to stress that the critiques offered above of certain forms of socialist theorizing are in *no sense* a defence of the 'anti-theory' positions still too common on the British Left (for example E.P. Thompson's *The Poverty of Theory*, which is brilliantly demolished in Hirst 1979b). But there is of course theory and theory. The kind of theoretical work which is desperately required is not the repetitive elaboration of general theories of social relations which is the staple of much if not most socialist theoretical work. Rather there is the need for the theorization in areas (such as markets, the theory of the enterprise) where socialist objectives can be specified but where those objectives are obstructed not only in their achievement but even in their precise formulation by the absence of adequate theory.

The need is not for a turning away from 'theory' (whatever exactly this might mean) but a certain theoretical iconoclasm. The theoretical basis of much Left discussion is unfortunately only too much an illustration of Marx's famous aphorism that 'The traditions of all dead generations weighs like a nightmare on the basis of the living.'

Finally the small amount of theoretical iconoclasm which this book has tried to develop does raise one difficult problem – where does it leave socialism, if many things which socialists have said appear so ill-conceived and if in addition general theories of social relations are to be so discarded? This is clearly a very large question indeed, but some brief points may be made to indicate that socialist politics *are* compatible with the stance of this book, albeit not perhaps in very traditional ways.

First socialist objectives must be treated as objectives formulated as desirable by socialists – not treated as the *objective* interests of the working class, nor as necessary outcomes in any historical process. Take the example of democracy in the enterprise. As argued above it is far from clear what democracy in the enterprise is a *means* to, and certainly unclear that it will realize any well-known worker interest (in relation to wages, hours, conditions of work, for example). Equally weak seems to be any suggestion that there is some kind of democratic imperative pushing out the frontiers of democracy from politics into the economy (cf. the Bullock Report).

Such a position *does* not mean that socialist objectives are utopian in the sense attacked in Marx's *Socialism: Utopian and Scientific*. This work postulates a socialism tied either to irreversible historical forces or to a belief that a simple statement of socialist truth by the enlightened would guarantee mass support. But this is not the only choice. We must take on board the Marxian stress on the complex economic and political conditions for the success of socialist politics whilst discarding any *necessary* links between economic structure and political change. Socialist politics does require definite material conditions of existence – trade unions, political parties, etc. – and these cannot be wished into existence. But equally their existence in no way guarantees socialist success.

Secondly socialist objectives can be specified in general ways: socialists have traditionally aspired to co-operative, egalitarian, democratic and non-commodity forms of social relations and these (with the possible exception of the last?) may be accepted, albeit provisionally. These objectives provide a *means of assessment* of

146

definite social arrangements – they give socialists some kind of bench-mark against which to judge possible changes in such social arrangements. But these objectives *do not* provide clear guides to the means for their attainment, and this again is an area crying out for theoretical work. For example there is remarkably little socialist work on democracy, which provides a starting point for political argument.

Lastly I have deliberately spoken of socialist objectives rather than socialism. This latter term carries too much of a connotation of a society organized around a single principle of social organization to be acceptable. Socialist politics are dominated by such notions, with the implication that there will be a day upon which something called 'socialism' will arrive. But this is clearly in danger of reverting back to those general theories of social relations which have been attacked in this book. This is not to deny that to talk of 'socialism' may be as politically unavoidable as talking about 'capitalist' enterprises, but it should only be done with a full awareness of the problems of such homogenizing categories.

NOTES

1 I owe this point directly to Stuart Burchell.
2 As the class *never* in fact acts as one, this always involves a postulate as to what class *interests* 'really are'.
3 The implication of this is not that socialists would support a 'free for all' in pursuit of jobs but that different objectives must be pursued at different levels, in particular full employment may not be an objective achievable by policy at the enterprise level alone (see on this Burchell and Tomlinson 1982).
4 In the United States there is an enormous literature (see especially the *Journal of Law and Economics* and the *Bell Journal of Economics and Management*) opposing regulation of private industry and commerce, and this has had notable political success. For a summary of the arguments see Stigler (1975). One of the problems with this literature is the ambiguity over whether the defects of regulation are intrinsic to any kind of regulation as the literature usually suggests or a consequence of particular modes of regulation. For example Posner (1974, pp. 349–50) asks how if all regulation is pernicious legal regulation by the judiciary of the market system can be beneficial, which he wants to argue it clearly is. The implication would seem to be that once *one* form of regulation is seen as potentially beneficial to the public interest, the bad effects of regulation cannot be seen as the emanation of the *essence* of a homogeneous state but conditioned by the particularities of each form of regulation. Regulation then may sin but it is not forever condemned by Original Sin.
5 See especially the Report on *The Rugby Portland Cement Company Ltd* (HC

346, HMSO 1979), on *Metal Box* (HC 135, HMSO 1978) and on *Allied Breweries* (HC415, HMSO 1978). Because of time and resource constraints the extent of company scrutinies by the Commission was much less than might be assumed from the vehemence of complaints against it.

6 See, for a comparable problem in British macroeconomic policy, Bryan Hopkin's discussion of demand management in Cairncross (1981, p. 35 *et seq.*).

7 It is slightly odd to see the pride of place given by Aaronovitch and Smith (1981, pp. 256–8) to the rather simple, formal investment appraisal calculations such as 'Net Present Value' at the expense of this kind of strategic assessment.

Bibliography

Unless otherwise stated, the place of publication is London.

Aaronovitch, S. (1955) *Monopoly*.

Aaronovitch, S. (1961) *The Ruling Class*.

Aaronovitch, S. (1981) *The Road from Thatcherism*.

Aaronovitch, S. and Sawyer, M. (1975) *Big Business*.

Aaronovitch, S. and Smith, R. (1981) *The Political Economy of British Capitalism*.

Addison, C. *et al.* (1933) *Problems of a Socialist Government*.

Babbage, C. (1835) *On the Economy of Machinery and Manufactures* (4th edn), reprinted New York, 1971.

Baran, P. and Sweezy, P. (1968) *Monopoly Capital*.

Barratt-Brown, M. (1958) 'The Insiders', *Universities and Left Review* (Winter).

Barratt-Brown, M. (1959) 'The Controllers', *Universities and Left Review*, 4.

Barratt-Brown, M. (1963) 'Crosland's Enemy', *New Left Review*, 19.

Barratt-Brown, M. (1968a) 'The Limits of the Welfare State', in K. Coates (ed.) *Can the Workers Run Industry?*

Barratt-Brown, M. (1968b) *Opening the Books*, Institute of Workers Control Pamphlet 4.

Barry, E. (1965) *Nationalisation in British Politics*.

Batstone, E. and Davies, P.L. (1976) *Worker Directors: European Experience*.

Berg, M. (ed.) (1979) *Technology and Toil in Nineteenth Century Britain*.

Berle, A. and Means, G. (1932) *The Modern Corporation and Private Property*.

Berman, K.V. (1967) *Worker-owned Plywood Companies*, Washington State.

Bettelheim, C. (1976) *Economic Calculation and Forms of Property*.

Bettelheim, C. and Sweezy, P. (1971) *On the Transition to Socialism*, New York.

Blackburn, R. (1972) 'The New Capitalism', in R. Blackburn (ed.) *Ideology in Social Science*.

Boston (1975): Boston Group Associates, *Strategy Alternatives for the British Motor Cycle Industry*.

Braverman, H. (1974) *Labour and Monopoly Capital*, New York.

Bray, J. and Falk, N. (1974) *Towards a Worker Managed Economy*, Fabian Tract 430.

Bright, J. (1958) 'Does Automation Raise Skill Requirements?', *Harvard Business Review*, 36 (4).

Brighton Labour Process Group (1977) 'The Capitalist Labour Process', *Capital and Class*, 1.

Brooke, M. and Van Beusekom, M. (1979) *International Corporate Planning*.

Brus, W. (1972) *The Market in a Socialist Economy*.

Bullock (1977) Committee of Enquiry into Industrial Democracy *Report*, Cmnd 6706.

Burchell, S. and Tomlinson, J. (1982) 'The AES, Control of Capital and the Enterprise', in T. Manwaring and J. Kelly (eds) *For Popular Socialism: the AES and Beyond*.

Burnham, J. (1940) *The Managerial Revolution*.

Cairncross, F. (ed.) (1981) *Changing Perceptions of Economic Policy*.

Castles, A. (1978) *The Social Democratic Image of Society*.

Chandler, A. (1962) *Strategy and Structure*, Harvard.

Channon, D. and Jalland, M. (1979) *Multinational Strategic Planning*.

Chester, D. (1952) 'Management and Accountability in the Nationalised Industries', *Public Administration*, xxx (Spring).

Child, J. (1969) *The Business Enterprise in Modern Industrial Society*.

Clarke, T. (1977) 'Industrial Democracy: the Institutionalised Suppression of Industrial Conflict', in T. Clarke and L. Clements (eds) *Trade Unions under Capitalism*.

Cliff, T. and Peterson, R. (1976) 'Portugal: the Last 3 Months', *International Socialism*, 87.

Clifton, J. (1977) 'Competition and the Evolution of the Capitalist Mode of Production', *Cambridge Journal of Economics*, 1 (2).

Coates, D. (1980) *Labour in Power?*

Coates, K. (1976) *The New Worker Co-operatives.*

Cole, G.D.H. (1919) *Self Government in Industry.*

Cole, G.D.H. (1920a) *Guild Socialism Restated.*

Cole, G.D.H. (1920b) 'Democracy in Industry', in P. Alden *et al.* (eds) *Labour in Industry.*

Cole, G.D.H. (1921) *Social Theory.*

Cole, G.D.H. (1929) *The Next Ten Years in British Social and Economic Policy.*

Cole, G.D.H. (1931) 'The Essentials of Socialisation', *Political Quarterly*, 2 (3).

Cole, G.D.H. (1932) *Economic Tracts for the Times.*

Cole, G.D.H. (1955) *Studies in Class Structure.*

Cole, M. (ed.) (1952) *Beatrice Webb's Diaries.*

Coutts, K., Godley, W. and Nordhaus, W. (1978) *Industrial Pricing in the U.K.*, Cambridge.

Coventry (1980): Coventry, Liverpool, Newcastle and North Tyneside Trades Councils *State Intervention in Industry: A Workers' Inquiry.*

Cowling, K. *et al.* (1980) *Mergers and Economic Performance*, Cambridge.

Crompton, R. and Gubbay, J. (1977) *Economy and Class Structure.*

Crosland, A. (1952) 'The Transition from Capitalism', in R. Crossman (ed.) *New Fabian Essays.*

Crosland, A. (1956) *The Future of Socialism.*

Crosland, A. (1962) *The Conservative Enemy.*

Crosland, A. (1966) 'The Private and Public Corporation in Great Britain', in E. Mason (ed.) *The Corporation in Modern Society.*

Crosland, A. (1974) *Socialism Now.*

Crossman, R. (1950) *Socialist Values in a Changing Civilisation*, Fabian Tract 286.

Crossman, R. (1952) *Socialism and the New Despotism*, Fabian Tract 298.

CSE/LWG (1980): Conference of Socialist Economists/London Working Group *The Alternative Economic Strategy.*

Cutler, A. (1978) 'The Romance of "Labour"', *Economy and Society*, 7 (1).

Cutler, A., Hindess, B., Hirst, P. and Hussain, A. (1977, 1978) *Marx's Capital and Capitalism Today* (2 vols).

Dahl, R. (1947) 'Workers' Control of Industry and the British Labour

Party', *American Political Science Review*, XLI, (October).

Dalton, J. and Penn, D. (1976) 'The Concentration-Profitability Relationship: Is There a Critical Concentration Ratio?', *Journal of Industrial Economics*, XXV (2).

Donzelot, J. (1980) *The Policing of Families*.

Eccles, T. (1981) *Under New Management*.

Edwards, R. (1980) *Contested Terrain*.

Eichner, A. (1976) *The Megacorp and Oligopoly*, Cambridge.

Elger, T. (1979) 'Valorisation and De-skilling: A Critique of Braverman', *Capital and Class*, 7.

Engles, F. (1892) 'On Authority,' in L. Feuer (ed.) *K. Marx and F. Engels: Basic Writings in Politics and Philosophy*.

Fabians (1976): A Fabian Group *Workers in the Boardroom*, Fabian Tract 441.

Faundez, J. and Piciotto, S. (eds) (1978) *The Nationalisation of Multinationals in Peripheral Economies*.

Fine, B. and O'Donnell, K. (1981) 'The Nationalised Industries', *Socialist Economic Review*.

Fishman, D. (1980) 'A Radical View of the European Monetary System', *Politics and Power*, 1.

Florence, P.S. (ed.) (1961) *Ownership, Control and Success of Large Companies*.

Fox, A. (1974) *Beyond Contract: Work, Power and Trust Relations*.

Fox, A. (1978) *Socialism and Shop Floor Power*, Fabian Research Series 338.

Francis, A. (1980) 'Families, Firms and Finance Capital: The Development of UK Industrial Firms with Particular Reference to Their Ownership and Control', *Sociology*, 14 (1).

Friedman, A. (1977) *Industry and Labour*.

Friedman, M. (1953) *Essays in Positive Economics*, Chicago.

Friedmann, G. (1964) *Industrial Society: The Emergence of Human Problems of Automation*, Glencoe, Ill.

Gaitskell, H. (1956) *Socialism and Nationalisation*, Fabian Tract 300.

Glyn, A. (1978) *Capitalist Crisis: Tribunes 'Alternative' Strategy or Socialist Plan*.

Glyn, A. and Sutcliffe, R. (1972) *British Capitalism, Workers and the Profit Squeeze*, Harmondsworth.

Goodman, E. (1969) *The Impact of Size*.

Gorz, A. (1978) 'The Tyranny of the Factory: Today and Tomorrow', in A. Gorz (ed.) *The Division of Labour*, Hassocks.

Gower, C. (1979) *Company Law* (4th edn).

Granick, D. (1976) *Enterprise Guidance in Eastern Europe*, Princeton.

Green, F. and Nore, P. (eds) (1977) *Economics: An Anti-Text*.

Hadden, T. (1977) *Company Law and Capitalism* (2nd edn).

Hall, M. and Winsten, C.B. (1959) 'The Ambiguous Notion of Efficiency', *Economic Journal*, 69.

Hanson, A. (1954) 'Labour and the Public Corporation', *Public Administration*, xxxii (Summer).

Hart, P.E. and Clarke, R. (1980) *Concentration in British Industry 1935–1975*.

Haseler, S. (1969) *The Gaitskellites*.

Hay, J. and Morris, D. (1980) *Industrial Economics*, Oxford.

Hayek, F. (ed.) (1935) *Collectivist Economic Planning*.

Hindess, B. (1977) 'Humanism and Teleology in Sociological Theory', in B. Hindess (ed.) *Sociological Theories of the Economy*.

Hindess, B. (1978) *Philosophy and Methodology in the Social Sciences*, Brighton.

Hindess, B. (1980) 'Democracy and the Limitations of Parliamentary Democracy in Britain', *Politics and Power*, 1.

Hinton, J. (1973) *The First Shop Stewards Movement*.

Hirsch, F. (1977) *The Social Limits to Growth*.

Hirst, P. (1978) 'Althusser and the Theory of Ideology', *Economy and Society*, 5 (4).

Hirst, P. (1979a) *On Law and Ideology*.

Hirst, P. (1979b) 'The Necessity of Theory', *Economy and Society*, 8 (4).

Hirst, P. (1980) 'Law, Socialism and Rights', in P. Carlen and M. Collison (eds) *Radical Issues in Criminology*.

Hirst, P. (1981a) 'Constructing the "Social"', *Politics and Power*, 3.

Hirst, P. (1981b) 'On Struggle in the Enterprise', in M. Prior (ed.) *The Popular and the Political*.

HMSO (1976) *Economic Trends* (August).

Hodges, J. and Hussain, A. (1979) 'Review Article: Jacques Donzelot', *Ideology and Consciousness*, 5.

Holland, S. (1976) *The Socialist Challenge*.

Holland, S. (ed.) (1978) *Beyond Capitalist Planning*.

Holmes, P. (1978) *Industrial Pricing Behaviour and Devaluation*.

Hussain, A. (1976) 'Hilfreding's Finance Capital', *Bulletin of the Conference of Socialist Economists* (June).

Hyman, R. (1974) 'Workers' Control and Revolutionary Socialism', *Socialist Register*.

153

Hyman, R. (1975) *Industrial Relations: A Marxist Introduction.*

Hyman, R. (1979) 'The Politics of Workplace Trade Unionism', *Capital and Class*, 8.

Ingham, G. (1974) *Strikes and Industrial Conflict: Britain and Scandinavia.*

International Socialism (1974): IS National Committee Policy Statement, *International Socialism*, 73 (December).

→ Katzarov, K. (1964) *The Theory of Nationalisation*, The Hague.

Keegan, J. (1976) *The Face of Battle*, Harmondsworth.

→ Kennet, W., Whitty, L. and Holland, S. (1971) *Sovereignty and Multinational Companies*, Fabian Tract 409.

Keynes, J. (1933) 'The Means to Prosperity', *Collected Writings* IV, *Essays in Persuasion.*

Labour Party (1918) *Report of the Annual Conference of the Labour Party.*

Labour Party (1932) *Report of the Annual Conference of the Labour Party.*

Labour Party (1959) *Report of the Annual Conference of the Labour Party.*

Labour Party (1974) *The Community and the Company: Reform of Company Law.*

Labour Party (1976) *Report of the Annual Conference of the Labour Party.*

Labour Party (1977) *International Big Business.*

Liberal Party (1928) *Britain's Industrial Future.*

Littlejohn, G. (1979) 'State, Plan and Market in the Transition to Socialism', *Economy and Society*, 8 (2).

McKibbin, R. (1974) *The Evolution of the Labour Party 1910–1924*, Oxford.

H. Macmillan (1938) *The Middle Way.*

Mandel, E. (1975) 'Self-Management – Dangers and Possibilities', *International 2* (4).

Marx, K. (1954) *Capital*, vol I.

Marx, K. (1972) *Capital*, vol. III.

Marx, K. (1974) 'Inaugural Address to the IWMA', in D. Fernbach (ed.) *The First International and After.*

Marx, K. and Engels, F. (1979) *Collected Works*, vol. 11.

Matthews, R. (1968) 'Why Has Britain Had Full Employment since the War?', *Economic Journal*, 78 (3).

→ Miliband, R. (1968) *The State in Capitalist Society.*

Miliband, R. (1973) *Parliamentary Socialism.*

Minns, R. (1980) *Pension Funds and British Capitalism.*

Minson, J. (1980) 'Strategies for Socialists? Foucault's Conception of Power', *Economy and Society*, 9.

Morrison, H. (1933) *Socialism and Transport.*

Morrison, H. (1959) *Government and Parliament.*

Mukherjee, S. (1972) *Making Labour Markets Work.*

Nelson, D. (1974) 'Scientific Management, Systematic Management and Labour', *Business History Review*, 48 (4).

Nelson, D. and Campbell, S. (1972) 'Taylorism versus Welfare Work in American Industry', *Business History Review*, 46 (1).

Nichols, T. (1969) *Ownership, Control and Ideology.*

Nichols, T. (1980) *Capital and Labour.*

Nichols, T. and Beynon, H. (1977) *Living with Capitalism.*

Nyman, S. and Silbertson, A. (1978) 'The Ownership and Control of Industry', *Oxford Economic Papers*, 30 (1).

Oakeshott, R. (1978) *The Case for Workers' Co-operatives.*

Owen, D. (1981) *Face the Future.*

Panitch, L. (1976) *Social Democracy and Industrial Militancy.*

Panitch, L. (1980) 'Recent Theorisations of Corporatism', *British Journal of Sociology*, XXXI (2).

Parker, S. (1975) 'Meriden and Workers' Control', *Revolutionary Communist*, 1.

Phillips, A. (1976) 'A Critique of Empirical Studies of Relations between Market Structure and Profitability', *Journal of Industrial Economics*, XXV (4).

Pitkin, H. (1967) *The Concept of Representation*, Berkeley.

Pollard, S. (1979) 'The Nationalisation of the Banks: The Chequered History of a Socialist Proposal', in D. Martin and D. Rubenstein (eds) *Ideology and the Labour Movement.*

Posner, M. (1974) *The Economic Analysis of Law*, Boston.

Postgate, R. (1920) *The Bolshevik Theory.*

Potter, B. (1891/1930) *The Co-operative Movement in Great Britain.*

Poulantzas, N. (1969) 'The Problem of the Capitalist State', *New Left Review*, 58.

Poulantzas, N. (1975) *Classes in Contemporary Capitalism.*

Prais, S. (1974) 'A New Look at the Growth of Industrial Concentration', *Oxford Economic Papers*, 26 (2).

Prais, S. (1976) *The Evolution of Giant Firms in Britain*, Cambridge.

Pratten, C. (1971) *Economies of Scale in Manufacturing Industry.*

Pribecevic, B. (1959) *The Shop Stewards Movement and Workers' Control.*

Ramelson, B. (1975) *Comment*, 13 (6).

Ramsay, H. (1977) 'Cycles of Control: Workers Participation in

Sociological and Historical Perspective', *Sociology*, 11 (3).

Reati, A. (1980) 'Capitalist Profit Calculation and Inflation Accounting: A Comment', *Economy and Society*, 9 (1).

Robson, W. (ed.) (1937) *Public Enterprise*.

Rose, N. (1977) 'Fetishism and Ideology', *Ideology and Consciousness*, 2.

Rose, N. (1980) 'Socialism and Social Policy: The Problems of Inequality', *Politics and Power*, 2.

Rowthorn, R. and Ward, T. (1980) 'How to Run a Company and Run Down an Economy', *Cambridge Journal of Economics*, 3.

Salaman, G. (1979) *Work Organisation: Resistance and Control*.

Salaman, G. (1981) *Class and the Corporation*.

Samuel, R. (1977) 'The Workshop of the World', *History Workshop Journal*, 3.

Sandilands (1975) *Inflation Accounting: Report of the Inflation Accounting Committee*, Cmnd 6225.

Scherer, F. (1980) *Industrial Market Structure and Economic Performance*, Chicago.

Schumacher, F. (1973) *Small Is Beautiful*.

Scott, J. (1979) *Corporations, Classes and Capitalism*.

Scott, J. and Hughes, M. (1976) 'Ownership and Control in a Satellite Economy: A Discussion from Scottish Data', *Sociology*, 10 (1).

Singh, A. (1977) 'UK Industry and the World Economy: A Case of De-Industrialisation?', *Cambridge Journal of Economics*, 1 (2).

Socialist Worker (1974) Editorial in *Socialist Worker*, 20 July.

Sparks, C. (1974) 'The Co-operative Solution: The NVT Experience', *International Socialism*, 73.

Speer, A. (1971) *Inside the Third Reich*.

Stigler, G. (1975) *The Citizen and the State: Essays on Regulation*, Chicago.

Strachey, J. (1956) *Contemporary Capitalism*.

Sweezy, P. (1968) *The Theory of Capitalist Development*, New York.

Tannenbaum, A.S., Kavcic, B., Rosner, M., Vianello, M. and Wieser, G. (1974) *Hierarchy in Organizations*, San Francisco.

Thompson, E. (1978) *The Poverty of Theory and Other Essays*.

Thompson, G. (1977) 'The Relationship Between the Financial and Industrial Sectors of the UK Economy', *Economy and Society*, 6 (3).

Thompson, G. (1978) 'Capitalist Profit Calculation and Inflation Accounting', *Economy and Society*, 7 (4).

Thornley, J. (1981) *Worker Co-ops: Jobs and Dreams*.

Tivey, L. (1978) *The Politics of the Firm*.

Tomlinson, J. (1980a) 'Socialist Politics and the "Small Business"', *Politics and Power*, 1.

Tomlinson, J. (1980b) 'British Politics and Co-operatives', *Capital and Class*, 12.

Tomlinson, J. (1981a) 'Corporatism: A Further Sociologisation of Marxism', *Politics and Power*, 4.

Tomlinson, J. (1981b) 'Why Was There Never a Keynesian Revolution in Economic Policy?', *Economy and Society*, 10 (1).

Tomlinson, J. (1981c) *Problems of British Economic Policy 1870–1945*.

TUC (1931) *Annual Report of the Trades Union Congress*.

TUC (1933) *Report of the Trades Union Congress for 1933*.

TUC (1935) *Report of the Trades Union Congress for 1935*.

TUC (1944) *Interim Report on Post-War Reconstruction*, Appendix to TUC Annual Report.

Ure, A. (1834) *The Philosophy of Manufactures*, reprinted 1967.

Vernon, R. (1977) *Storm over the Multinationals*, Harvard.

Webb, B. and S. (1914) 'Associations of Producers', Special Supplement to the *New Statesman* (14 February).

Webb, B. and S. (1920a) *History of Trade Unionism*.

Webb, B. and S. (1920b) *Industrial Democracy*.

Westergard, J. and Resler, H. (1975) *Class in a Capitalist Society*.

Williams, N. (1979) 'The Profitability of UK Industrial Sectors', *Bank of England Quarterly Bulletin*, 19 (4).

Williamson, H.F. (ed.) (1975) *Evolution of International Management Structures*, Newark, Delaware.

Winter, S. (1964) 'Economic Natural Selection and the Theory of the Firm', *Yale Economic Essays*, 4 (1).

Winyard, S. (1976) *Policing Low Wages*, Low Pay Unit, Pamphlet 4.

Worker Directors (1977) *Worker Directors Speak*, Farnborough.

Wright, A. (1979) *G.D.H. Cole and Socialist Democracy*, Oxford.

Zeitlin, M. (1974) 'Corporate Ownership and Control: The Large Corporation and the Capitalist Class', *American Journal of Sociology*, 73.

Index